4/03

DATE			

WEALTH AND OUR COMMONWEALTH

Wealth and Our Commonwealth

Why America Should Tax Accumulated Fortunes

WILLIAM H. GATES SR.

AND CHUCK COLLINS

Beacon Press

BOSTON

336. 276
GAT

Beacon Press
25 Beacon Street
Boston, Massachusetts 02108-2892
www.beacon.org

Beacon Press books
are published under the auspices of
the Unitarian Universalist Association of Congregations.

06 05 04 03   8 7 6 5 4 3 2

This book is printed on acid-free paper that meets the uncoated paper
ANSI / NISO specifications for permanence as revised in 1992.

Composition by Wilsted & Taylor Publishing Services

Library of Congress Cataloging-in-Publication Data
Gates, William H.
    Wealth and our commonwealth : why America should tax accumulated
fortunes / William H. Gates Sr., and Chuck Collins.
        p.   cm.
Includes bibliographical references.
    ISBN 0-8070-4718-X (hardcover : alk. paper)
    1. Inheritance and transfer tax—United States.   I. Collins, Chuck.
    II. Title.
    HJ5805. G38 2003
    336.2'76'0973—dc21
                                                            2002011326

To Bill Gates III, my son, whose hard work and generosity made estate taxation relevant to me; and to Kristi Blake and Libby Armintrout, my daughters, who are understanding about my wanting the United States to share in their inheritance. —W. H. G. Sr.

To Edward J. Collins, my father, for his gifts of love and curiosity. —C. C.

CONTENTS

Paul A. Volcker

I didn't get it last year.

I still don't get it.

Why, right now, in the aftermath of the greatest burst of paper wealth creation in all of American history (in all of history for all I know), in the midst of growing concern (even alarm) about the growing disparity of wealth and income in the United States, right in the face of increasing pressures on the federal budget, has there been so much effort to abolish the estate tax?

Reform—long overdue—I can understand. But total *elimination* of a tax broadly accepted as a reasonable part of our revenue system for close to a century is quite another thing.

Of course, no one likes to pay taxes when alive, or at the expense of potential heirs, after death. But I think we all recognize, liberal or conservative, rich or poor, that some taxes, like death itself, are inevitable. The unavoidable fact is that government has certain responsibilities. The discharge of those responsibilities costs money.

We can, we should, and we endlessly do debate just how far those governmental responsibilities should extend, and how much we should spend. We should also be careful about how we tax. We want to minimize adverse effects on incentives. We should be watchful about distorting economic activity in ways that reduce efficiency, productivity, and growth.

What we can't escape is a simple piece of logic. Once we agree on total expenditures and revenues, if we lose one existing source of revenue—say from the federal estate tax—we will have to find a replacement. That will become harder and harder to do a few years ahead, when estate tax revenues will likely increase rapidly, reflecting the enormous rise in wealth during the 1980s and 1990s. It's hard for me—hard in terms of economic analysis—to think of practical alternatives with fewer adverse effects than a (reformed) estate tax.

Consider the main possibilities. More points on the income tax, directly contrary to "supply-side" theorizing? New sales or value-added taxes, regressive in their impact on already skewed incomes? Even if we succeed, right against the current trend, in reducing total spending and revenue needs, we would still have to choose among various taxes. Quite apart from questions of political practicality, we would be hard-pressed to find evidence that, compared with the alternatives, a reasonable estate tax significantly discourages work effort or innovation or savings.

I realize much more is at stake than these calculations of the "dismal science" of economics.

In *Wealth and Our Commonwealth,* Bill Gates Sr. and Chuck Collins appeal to one of the more treasured and persistent strains in the uniquely American experience. From the days of our founding fathers, through Democratic and Republican administrations, among conservatives and liberals alike, the concept of equality of opportunity and dispersion of wealth and economic power has been a part of the American psyche. The inheritance of huge fortunes, far beyond any reasonable need for education, for medical care, and for a comfortable—even luxurious—standard of living has never rested easily with that political philosophy.

Of course, money is not the only measure of real wealth and opportunity, and perhaps not the most important. Moreover, some monetary measure of equality at the starting gate of life will never be achieved, certainly not by taxation, and it wouldn't make sense to try. But surely, as the authors so eloquently set out, our traditional values—our moral values—should weigh heavily, in fact conclusively, on the side of *some* tax on exceptionally large estates.

Plainly, the act hastily passed in 2001, with a sudden phaseout in 2010 only to be reversed the following year, doesn't make sense.

Black humor about the incentives to keep grandma on the respirator until the turn of the year is only a macabre exaggeration of the enormous complications for rational estate planning of the existing law. The added burdens implicit for strained state budgets is only one of the poorly foreseen "side effects."

The time has come for real reform, sustainable reform, that deals with outdated and unnecessarily intrusive elements of the old and new laws. For one thing, we ought to take account of inflation and the rising levels of real wealth. Gates and Collins rightly suggest the old six-hundred-thousand-dollar and the current million-dollar exemptions are too low. A swath of families that today would be considered among the reasonably affluent rather than the exceptionally wealthy are affected. Similarly the annual allowances for individual tax-free gifts, now eleven thousand dollars, could be raised significantly. The purported adverse impact on family farms and small family business—which Gates and Collins convincingly document as enormously exaggerated by propagandists for the end of "death taxes"—could be practically eliminated.

But by all means let's keep the tax on truly huge fortunes. Even then, no one would be forced to pay over any of his or her estate to government against his or her wishes. Instead, an exemption for charitable institutions provides other avenues for satisfying personal and community objectives.

This book sets out one reasonable approach toward reform. No doubt others can and will be suggested. What strikes me as insupportable—insupportable as a matter of fiscal and economic analysis and insupportable in terms of a simple fairness and traditional American values—is to abolish the estate tax altogether. I am confident that that conclusion is shared by many thousands of business leaders and extremely wealthy individuals whose estates will be subject to tax. I am confident that there is support among the broader population. It is those voices that seem to me in touch with long-held American values and ideals. And it is those voices, the "silent majority," that need to be heard as the political attack on the estate tax is renewed.

On Valentine's Day, 2001, a front-page article in the *New York Times* sent a tremor through America's political elite. A prominent group of millionaires and billionaires had publicly launched a petition in opposition to wholesale repeal of the estate tax, our nation's only tax on accumulated wealth.

The initial supporters included financier George Soros, actor Paul Newman, art patron Agnes Gund, several members of the Rockefeller family, and other business leaders. Investor Warren Buffett chose not to sign the statement because he felt it did not go far enough in defending the estate tax—but went publicly on the record opposing repeal.

The effort, organized by the Boston-based Responsible Wealth, caught people's imagination and interest. Within weeks, over one thousand high-net-worth individuals, business leaders, and entrepreneurs, all of whom would someday pay estate taxes, added their names to support the cause.[1]

It is not surprising that the "billionaire backlash," as *Newsweek* called it, captured widespread attention, not only in the United States but around the world. If there were ever a "man bites dog" news story, this was it. An organized backlash of wealthy people, combined with the newsworthy and eternal themes of death, loss, legacy, taxation, wealth, and power, made for an irresistible story.

Responsible Wealth had spent six weeks preparing its Call to Preserve the Estate Tax. The statement's release had just the impact the group had hoped. At the eleventh hour, as estate tax repeal was about to be steamrolled through Congress, Responsible Wealth had hit the pause button. For the next several months, there was greater scrutiny of the shaky case for repeal. A movement to preserve the tax came together and began to frame a defense for reforming the tax, not abolishing it. This effort also contributed to a long overdue conversation about the dangers of concentrated wealth and power in a democratic society.

Why devote an entire book to a single provision of the tax code? The estate tax doesn't just raise revenue. The estate tax issue raises questions central to our democracy and our very identity as Americans. We agree with the sentiments of former IRS commissioner Sheldon Cohen: "People think taxation is a terribly mundane subject. But what makes it fascinating is that taxation, in reality, is life. If you know the position a person takes on taxes, you can tell their whole philosophy. The tax code, once you get to know it, embodies all the essence of life: greed, politics, power, goodness, charity. Everything's in there."[2]

The estate tax has it all: life and death, our beliefs about success, our attitudes about government, and our struggles over the character of American civic and economic life. It also includes an implicit assumption about society's claim on accumulated wealth.

Just what is the estate tax? The estate tax is a transfer tax imposed on large accumulations of wealth when someone dies. Its exemptions are so high that it falls on the heirs of fewer than 2 percent of estates every year. It contains provisions that encourage charitable giving—and favor the transfer of businesses and farms if they remain family-owned and -operated.

The estate tax helps make America great. The estate tax distinguishes this country from Europe and other countries with vestiges of aristocracies. There is something fundamentally American about the notion that what people do with their lives is more important than the station of birth. Don't we glory in the economic mobility that exists in America, as imperfect as it is? Don't we treasure the stepping stones we have built toward the ideal of equality of opportunity? Haven't we a collective distaste for the trappings of monarchy, and a healthy distrust of inherited wealth and privilege? The estate tax is no marginal issue. The estate tax connects us to our country's most fundamental values.

THE ESTATE TAX: IS IT GONE?

On June 7, 2001, President George W. Bush signed into law the Economic Growth and Tax Relief Reconciliation Act of 2001. Included in this tax bill was a reduction of income tax rates, a doubling of the child exemption, and—eventually—repeal of the estate tax that was instituted in 1916.

The overall tax bill, with its ten-year price tag of $1.35 trillion, was hastily pushed through both branches of Congress as the president's top domestic policy priority. Its proponents understood that for a number of reasons there was a brief political and economic window of opportunity.

This 2001 tax bill almost didn't happen. In the spring of 2001, with each passing day, the folly of this tax package was coming to light. The more the public understood how the tax cuts were tilted to benefit the wealthy and how they mortgaged the future, the less they liked them. Opposition was mounting and eroding support for the legislation. In retrospect, had Vermont senator James Jeffords defected from the Republican Party a week earlier, this tax bill might never have become law.[3]

The 2001 tax cut was marketed as an economic stimulus in the face of an optimistic ten-year $5.6 trillion budget surplus projection. We could do it all, we were told: cut taxes, protect Social Security, maintain national spending priorities, and reduce the deficit. But as the clouds of recession gathered on the horizon, the rosy assessment shifted and federal budget surplus estimates started to plummet. Within weeks of the tax cut's passage, congressional and administration budget counters dramatically reduced their surplus estimates.[4]

After the terrorist attacks on September 11, 2001, the country began spending significant amounts of money to address new defense needs. In addition to the rising expenditures of a global war against terrorism, our nation also made greater commitments to domestic law enforcement and security, airline bailouts, and the rebuilding of New York City. Congress debated an expensive economic stimulus package to address the recession, and red ink started to accumulate at a dizzying pace. By November 2001, the ten-year $5.6 trillion budget surplus that had been forecast had vanished and was replaced with government projections predicting four years of budget deficits. If the vote had taken place later, the 2001 tax cut would not have been enacted—and the estate tax would not have been earmarked for elimination.

Under the new law, complete repeal of the estate tax doesn't happen until January 1, 2010. Over the intervening years, the top rate drops from 55 percent to 45 percent and the amount of wealth exempted from the tax increases from $675,000 to $3.5 million. In one of the most amazing provisions of this law (or any other law) the entire 2001 tax bill is rescinded on January 1, 2011, and reverts back to the way it was in May 2001.[5] As a result, the estate tax is repealed for only one year, from January 1, 2010, to January 1, 2011, posing interesting planning questions and macabre family situations. One commentator speculated on the number of elder relations that will either be kept on life support until 2010 or suffer mysterious accidents during the 2010 calendar year.[6]

The 2001 tax bill was structured in this bizarre manner in order to wedge all of its expensive provisions into a congressionally mandated budget framework. In other words, Congress needed to shoehorn what would be a $1.776 trillion plus tax cut once it was fully phased in over ten years into a $1.35 trillion framework.[7] Like a magician's act, the tax bill deploys a curious assortment of phase-ins, phaseouts, and delayed activation dates and culminates with the ultimate disappearing act. Naturally, this was not a satisfying remedy for proponents of abolishing the estate tax, nor was it for those who support retention of some form of the tax.

Several times during 2002, the proponents of repeal put forward legislation to make the repeal permanent. On June 12, 2002, after easily passing the House, the permanent repeal provision fell short of the sixty votes required in the Senate. As this book goes to press, there may be other efforts to push the repeal provision in the fall of 2002.

The most troubling aspect of the passage of the 2001 tax bill was the lack of honest debate about the implications of repealing the estate tax. The proponents of repeal perpetuated a number of false assertions. They spent millions of dollars on advertising spin, constructing a mythology about the estate tax that went largely unchallenged in the media and the public square.

Why are we having this debate in the first place? Who shoved estate tax repeal onto our nation's already crowded political agenda? Not the American public. The most recent polling shows that tax cuts are among the lowest priorities for the vast majority of voters. In terms of tax cuts, repealing the estate tax is the least popular.[8] Estate tax repeal is on the agenda only because the estate tax offends the sensibilities of some very wealthy individuals and hefty campaign contributors.

We need an estate tax precisely for the reason that estate tax repeal has become a political issue in the first place. In a self-governing democracy, we should be alarmed when the power of concentrated wealth attempts to shape the terms of policy debate and dictate the rules of our society.

A more robust deliberation would discuss questions such as these:

- How much revenue would repeal of the estate tax lose in the future? What would be the trade-offs from losing $850 billion in revenue over the next twenty years? Couldn't this money be used to shore up Social Security over the longer term?
- At a time when state governments are cutting budgets, what would be the fiscal impact of estate tax repeal on states?
- What would be the impact on private charity? How would repeal affect the independent nonprofit sector, such as local hospitals, universities, land conservancies, and scientific research?

There are also broader social questions that are central to our understanding of the origins and importance of the estate tax.

- How might repeal contribute to further aggregations of wealth and power? What impact would increased inequality have on our democracy?
- What social harms might arise from the concentration of wealth in the same family for successive generations? When

does the concentration of wealth in a few hands begin to distort democratic institutions and undermine the common
good?

- What is the role of society and our communities in creating
and maintaining institutions that enable individuals to amass
wealth? What role does public investment play in the creation
of wealth? What return on society's investment is justified?

- What responsibility does our country have to correct gross in-
equities that potentially undermine equality of opportunity?

- What is the responsibility of wealthy individuals to their communities and country? What should be their attitude about
taxation?

Our country urgently needs to foster and deepen a rigorous
debate about these questions, similar to the debate our nation had
one hundred years ago that led to the establishment of an estate
tax.

CHAPTER ONE

What Kind of Nation Do We Want to Be?

The reality is that US society is polarizing and its social arteries hardening. The sumptuousness and bleakness of the respective lifestyles of rich and poor represent a scale of difference in opportunity and wealth that is almost medieval—and a standing offense to the American expectation that everyone has the opportunity for life, liberty and happiness.

—Will Hutton, *Observer of London*[1]

The purpose of the estate tax is not to raise revenue . . . but to gradually correct the distribution of wealth and to prevent concentrations of power detrimental to the fair value of political liberty and fair equality of opportunity.

—John Rawls, *A Theory of Justice*

What makes America great are the things we have done to strengthen equality of opportunity. Over the last century, we have made significant progress toward this ideal.

One of the important things our country has done to strengthen equality of opportunity is to put a brake on the accumulation of hereditary wealth. It could be argued that a society based on opportunity for all could still flourish in a nation with great inequalities of wealth. We share a concern with our nation's founders that the existence of a powerful economic aristocracy distorts our democracy and negates equality of opportunity. As we'll see, these fears were realized during the Gilded Age of the late 1800s, and the estate tax was part of our country's remedy.

The estate tax both limits the power of concentrated wealth and generates revenue to pay for government from those most able to pay. Our basic assumption in opposing repeal of the estate tax is that we will continue to have a federal government that will require substantial revenue. This assumption is not an argument—it is a plain and simple reality. Despite divergent views on the purpose and size of government, it is most reasonable that the estate tax be part of financing it.

But let's say, for the sake of argument, we agree that to pay for the minimal services of our federal government we need to raise a trillion dollars a year. Do we primarily raise this revenue from the incomes and wages of workers? Or from taxes on the consumption of goods? Or from the estates of deceased wealthy people? All taxes have upsides and downsides. Taxes that fall entirely on consumption discourage spending, thereby affecting the economy negatively. A tax system that raises revenue solely from income taxes would seriously burden persons with low incomes. An established principle of taxation is that a good tax system will raise revenue from a variety of sources and be fair, stable, and sufficient.

REVENUE LOSS AND THE TAX BURDEN SHIFT

The debate over the estate tax must take into account the absolute requirement for federal and state revenue. And the estate tax should be evaluated against all the other forms of taxation. What other form of taxation do we have that is better targeted to those most able to pay? No other constituency is in a better position to contribute to public services than the heirs of deceased multimillionaires. Although the progressive income tax collects revenue from those with high annual incomes, it does not begin to tap the reservoirs of vast wealth and assets that exist in our nation.

One way or another, a certain amount of money must be paid in taxes to the U.S. government to support its activities. We could have a long debate about the proper size and scope of government, but most people would agree that the federal government fulfills vital functions and we need to support its activities with tax dollars. Eliminating the estate tax would deprive the government of a dependable and highly progressive source of revenue.

As we'll see, the long-term fiscal health of the country has been put at risk by the 2001 tax cut. If that tax cut is not reversed, we can look forward to substantial budget deficits for decades to come. In this light, the elimination of the estate tax—and the shift in tax burden—is even more stark. As William Gale and Samara Potter noted in their assessment of the entire 2001 tax bill,

> Tax cuts are not simply a matter of returning unneeded or unused funds to taxpayers, but rather a choice to require other, future taxpayers to cover the long-term deficit, which the tax cut significantly exacerbates. Likewise, the notion that the surplus is "the taxpayers' money" and should be returned to them omits the observation that the fiscal gap is "the taxpayers' debt" and should be paid by them. Thus, the issue is not whether taxpayers should have their tax payments returned, but rather *which* taxpayers—current or future—will be required to pay for the spending obligations incurred by current and past taxpayers.[2]

Consider these looming budget deficits juxtaposed with the immense increases in personal wealth that have taken place in this country in the last fifteen to twenty years. Despite the instability in the stock market and the return to earth of the technology sector, there has been a dizzying accumulation of wealth.

It would be folly for the patchwork of future federal revenue sources not to include a tax on these accumulations. Today the revenue from the estate tax generates about $30 billion, or about 1 percent of federal revenue, but it could be a significant and larger contributor to the national revenue base in the years to come.

Boston College researchers John J. Havens and Paul G. Schervish have modeled projections about the scale of the intergenerational transfer of wealth that will occur between now and 2052.[3] They have also speculated about the scale of potential estate tax revenue. In their research, they offer a range of estimates based on different expectations of growth. The estimated size of the intergenerational transfer of wealth between 1998 and 2052 ranges from a low estimate of $40.6 trillion, based on a modest 2 percent growth rate, to a high estimate of $136.2 trillion, based on a 4 percent growth rate. Under the low growth estimate, an estimated $15.4 trillion will pass from the 839,000 estates valued at more than $5 million.[4]

Havens and Schervish estimate that over this period between $13.4 trillion and $25.8 trillion will pass from living parents to children. They estimate that the total bequests to heirs, including these inter vivos (between the living) gifts, will range from $24.6 trillion to $65.3 trillion. An estimated $19.4 trillion to $50.6 trillion will be given to charities.

The amount of revenue generated for the estate tax is substantial under these scenarios, even if we anticipate the impact of current reforms such as increased exemptions. Havens and Schervish project that under their low-growth estimate $8.5 trillion of this intergenerational wealth transfer will be paid in estate taxes. Over fifty-four years, average annual estate tax revenue would be $157 billion a year. Under the higher-growth estimate, estate tax revenue would be $40.6 trillion, for average annual estate tax revenue of $752 billion per year.

An estate tax on only the four hundred wealthiest Americans would generate substantial revenue. The average net worth of the individuals and families listed on the Forbes 400 is $2.4 billion. To join the 400 club required $725 million in 2001. This is a great leap from when *Forbes Magazine* first started counting in 1982, when the average net worth of the Forbes 400 was $400 million and the entry threshold was $91 million.[5] A meaningful estate tax imposed on these wonderfully successful people's wealth (their heirs, actually) could generate, at an effective tax rate of 30 percent and an exemption of $3 million, $278 billion over the years between now and the demise of the last survivor!

Losing federal estate tax revenue ranging from $157 billion to $752 billion a year would trigger two possible negative scenarios. There will be either serious cutbacks in public expenditures or serious increases in the taxes of those less able to pay.

THE IMPACT ON STATE TREASURIES

Estate and inheritance taxes at the state level preceded the current federal estate tax, but since the mid-1920s there has been an interaction between states and the federal government related to estate taxation. In 1926, the estate tax law was amended to allow taxpayers to claim a deduction against their federal estate tax liability for the amount of estate taxes they pay to their states.

Although estate tax repeal does not occur until the year 2010, some state governments are already beginning to feel the loss in revenue. In structuring the phaseout of the estate tax, congressional tax writers reduced the pinch on the federal treasury by accelerating the timetable of revenue loss to the states. Starting in 2002, thirty-eight states began to lose a portion of the revenue that they received through their state "pickup" tax.

Many states will lose all of this tax revenue sharing by 2005, while the repeal of the federal estate tax occurs more gradually over ten years. This structuring will accelerate the loss of at least $50 billion to $100 billion over the next ten years, about 1.5 percent of state tax collections. One of the ways the federal government masked the true costs of repeal was to shift this burden to the states. In essence, the federal government will end up pocketing the money that otherwise would have gone to the states from 2006 through 2011.

This is not chump change, especially for cash-strapped state legislatures. The impact on individual states varies by the size of the state and the wealth of its elderly population. California will lose the most in terms of dollars, with an estimated $356 million annual loss as the estate tax begins to be phased out in 2002—and a $1 billion loss by 2005, when it is fully phased out. For California, with the biggest state budget in the country, this accounts for only 1.2 percent of the state's total revenues. In New York, New Jersey, and Connecticut, each state would lose between 2.5 and 2.8 percent of total revenue. New Hampshire, which has no income tax on wages and no sales tax, would be the hardest hit. The $25 million loss would account for 4.6 percent of all state revenues.

Estate tax repeal couldn't come at a worse time for states. "This is going to hit at an especially hard time," wrote Kevin Sack in the *New York Times*, "as states are already facing declining revenues from sales taxes, income taxes and slumping capital gains. And they are facing further reductions in spending on schools, roads, prisons and social services." Some states are tapping rainy-day funds that they built up during the 1990s economic expansion.[6]

"The strong fiscal conditions of a year ago have been replaced by anemic revenue growth and expanding budget gaps," concluded a report by the National Conference of State Legislatures. "While revenue has slowed," writes John Harwood in the *Wall Street Journal*, "states have faced Medicaid health-care expenditures that rose by about 14%, more than double the rate forecast, in 40 states that the conference surveyed. As a result, state budget surpluses for the just-completed fiscal year fell by the largest proportion in 20 years, to 8.2% of spending from 11.5 percent in 2000."[7]

As states grapple with new constraints, they will be losing one of the most progressive sources of revenue available to them. Yet many people will not understand that one of the factors contributing to their woes is the repeal of the federal estate tax.

Instead, states will turn to the usual menu of possible budget cuts or revenue raisers. If they have the political will to raise revenue, which very few states do these days, they will probably not try to pass or expand a state inheritance tax, though some are considering ways to retain their state-level estate taxes.[8] In most cases, we will see increased sales and cigarette taxes, state income taxes, and cute accounting and revenue gimmicks, such as borrowing against future tobacco settlements and lotteries.

Even more likely, we will see budget cuts that trim very close to home, cuts that will affect the quality of public safety, schools, health care, and social services for the needy. The lost revenue from the repeal of the federal estate tax will most likely appear as an invisible gap, yet it will be another reason to tighten state and federal fiscal belts.

THE ESTATE TAX AND INEQUALITY

Preserving our federal estate tax plays a critical role in limiting the concentration of wealth in our country. It's surprising how little the recent debate over the estate tax probed this fundamentally American concern.

At the heart of the "American experiment" is our vision of equality of opportunity and the rejection of hereditary wealth and power. As inadequate as our efforts to build equality of opportunity have been, the establishment of greater concentrations of wealth and power will only undermine them.

America's democratic tradition is skeptical of concentrated wealth and power. What each of us *does* in our lives, our contribution to work and society, is thought to be more important than the family into which we are born.

When the estate tax was established in 1916, our nation was deep in struggle over the values of equality of opportunity versus hereditary privilege. The accumulation of great wealth and the power of the great trusts lead to questions about the direction of our society. One of the expressed intentions of the tax, as articulated by Theodore Roosevelt, was to break up "those fortunes swollen beyond all healthy limits."[9]

This sentiment was not "antirich." Rather, it branched out from a belief that such concentrations of wealth are corrosive to liberty. Today the levels of inequality in the United States are at their highest point since the 1920s.[10] This is an unusually imprudent time to abolish one of the few taxes that has slowed this buildup of wealth in the hands of a few.

THE DANGERS OF INEQUALITY TODAY

Our nation has presently attained levels of inequality approaching the 1880–1900 Gilded Age conditions that gave rise to a movement to establish the estate tax. Yet, after a pitifully one-sided debate, our response has been to eliminate one of the few mechanisms to correct this imbalance.

A recently observed slogan says it all: "I lived through ten years of unprecedented economic prosperity and all I got was this lousy T-shirt." The economic boom of the 1990s was highly uneven, with the majority of people's incomes staying flat. Over the last thirty years, real wages have remained largely stagnant or have fallen for the bottom 60 percent of households. In 1996, real wages started to climb so that by the year 2000 the median wage earner had almost climbed out of a hole. But after a two-decade long wage slump, the median wage earned in 2000 was still less, adjusting for inflation, than the median wage in 1973, when Richard Nixon was president.[11]

The United States is now the most unequal society in the industrialized world. The richest fifth of Americans earn eleven times more than the bottom fifth.[12] At the bottom end of the pay scale, the number of people working for poverty wages is troubling. The estimated "living wage," meant to lift a wage earner out of poverty, is now at least ten dollars an hour; the federal minimum wage is stalled at just over half that amount.[13] Many workers have held their households together by working longer hours, holding several jobs, and increasing the number of paid earners in their families. Two-paycheck families became the majority in 1998.[14] One cartoonist illustrated this development by depicting a politician speaking at a banquet, bragging that his "administration had created millions of new jobs." The waiter at the banquet observes, "Yes I know, I have three of them."

At the same time, the incomes of the top one-fifth of households increased steeply and the incomes of the top 1 percent have skyrocketed. The compensation gap between the highest-paid workers and those earning the average wage in the United States has grown at a dizzying pace. According to *Business Week*'s annual review of executive compensation, in 1980 the disparity between the highest-paid workers in America's 365 largest companies and their employees was forty-two to one. Today, the ratio exceeds five hundred to one.[15]

The disparities in wealth and savings are even more disturbing than income inequalities. Wealth ownership is a less visible yet critical indicator of economic well-being. Wealth is the security that people have to fall back on, the reserves that help them to weather an economic downturn. Savings and assets propel people forward to home ownership and small business development.

Historically, the share of private wealth owned by the top 1 percent of households has fluctuated. In 1870, before the peak of the Industrial Revolution, it is estimated that the wealthiest 1 percent owned 27 percent of wealth, with the top 10 percent owning 70 percent. By 1912, as the Gilded Age waned, the share owned by the top 1 percent had doubled to 56.4 percent. At the same time, the wealthiest 10 percent of households owned 90 percent of all wealth.[16] On the eve of the Great Depression, in 1928 and 1929, after the advent of modern taxation and the First World War, from 1914 through 1918, the share owned by the top 1 percent had declined to 40 percent of all private wealth.[17]

In the three decades after World War II, our nation actively pursued public policies that shared prosperity and equality of opportunity. The result was a greatly expanded middle class and reduced wealth inequality. These policies included the GI bill, federal mortgage assistance programs, college loans and grants, and incentives for small business development. These were costly initiatives that were paid for, in part, by progressive taxes.[18] Few people today would question the prudence of those investments, as many families celebrated their first home purchase and first college graduate in the postwar years.

The data about postwar years demonstrate that these were decades of relatively greater shared prosperity.[19] Incomes for all quintiles doubled between 1947 and 1979. It is estimated that by 1976 the share of wealth owned by the top 1 percent of households had dipped below 20 percent. Since then our society has reversed direction and moved toward levels of wealth inequality unparalleled since the eve of the Great Depression.

Today the wealthiest 1 percent of households again own over 38 percent of all private wealth. In terms of financial wealth, including the ownership of stocks, bonds, and other investments, the top 1 percent of households own 47 percent and the top 20 percent own 91 percent. The benefits of the economic boom of the last two decades were highly skewed to the top. Between 1983 and 1998, almost all the growth in wealth of the economic boom went to the top 20 percent of households. Over the same time period the wealth of the bottom 40 percent of households showed an absolute decline.[20]

It is true that more Americans than ever own stock. Since 1983, the percentage of Americans owning stock grew dramatically from 24.4 percent to 48.2 percent. This was the result of households shifting savings from banks to mutual funds and greater investment in retirement instruments, such as private pension accounts like 401(k) plans and IRAs. But even for those families with investments in the stock market, their stake was small. Only 32 percent of households owned more than ten thousand dollars in stock. The concentration of stock ownership mirrored the overall levels of wealth inequality, with the top 1 percent of the population owning 42 percent of all stock and the top 20 percent owning almost 90 percent.[21]

As more asset wealth was held in fewer hands, the savings rate went into steep decline, from 10.9 percent in 1982 to 2.3 percent in 2001.[22] With wage rates flat or falling, many Americans took on unprecedented amounts of consumer and mortgage debt.

The disparities in wealth are even more pronounced from the perspective of race. The median white household has eight times as much wealth as the median black household. The median net worth for a white household is $81,700; for African-Americans it is $10,000. Median Hispanic net worth declined from $5,300 in 1995 to $3,000 in 1998. Removing home ownership from the equation, white financial net worth is $37,600; African-American net worth is $1,200, and Hispanic financial net worth is $0, meaning half of Hispanic households have zero or negative financial net worth.[23]

No one can fully explain the causes of accelerating income and wealth inequality. But most economists agree that multiple forces are at work, including technological change, deunionization, and global competition. Public policies during this period, particularly taxation, have exacerbated inequalities by favoring large-asset owners and corporations over wage earners and smaller businesses. The taxation burden on higher incomes and capital gains has consistently fallen in the last four decades, shifting the tax burden off of high earners and large corporations and onto individual taxpayers.[24] The effort to repeal the estate tax is part of this trend.

Why does inequality matter? Some commentators have made the case that we should focus our efforts on alleviating poverty, not inequality. For this reason, a tremendous amount of public and charitable resources go toward lifting the floor, building pathways out of poverty for individuals and communities. But inequality does matter, because concentrations of wealth and power distort our democratic institutions and economic system and undermine social cohesion.

CONCENTRATED WEALTH AND DEMOCRACY

If concentrations of wealth did not translate into political power and influence in our democracy, they might be less troubling. But unfortunately they go hand in hand. As Supreme Court Justice Louis Brandeis observed a century ago, "We can have concentrated wealth in the hands of a few or we can have democracy. But we cannot have both."[25]

Once a household accumulates wealth above a certain threshold, say $15 million, it has moved beyond the point of meeting its needs and aspirations of itself and its heirs. Such households are now in the nation's top quarter of the richest 1 percent of households and stand atop a global pinnacle of wealth almost too enormous to contemplate. By the late 1990s, there were an estimated forty thousand households with more than $25 million and five thousand with over $100 million.[26] They may be asking themselves, as Bud Fox queried speculator Gordon Gekko in the 1987 film *Wall Street*, "How many yachts can you water-ski behind?"

The amassing of great wealth, above a certain point, becomes an accumulation of social and political power. This is not inherently evil power, as the legacy of Carnegie's libraries and Rockefeller's contributions to medical research attest. But in a democratic, self-governing society, we should be concerned with the potential threat that concentrated wealth poses to our democratic institutions. Political scientist Samuel Huntington observed that in the United States "money becomes evil not when it is used to buy goods but when it is used to buy power. . . . Economic inequalities become evil when they are translated into political inequalities."[27]

Our democracy is now at risk because of the enormous power of accumulated wealth. The practices of government, administration, and law writing have been molded by the money power of the few, against the interests of the many. For example, the concentration of media ownership narrows and cheapens public discourse. When Ben Bagdikian wrote *The Media Monopoly* in 1983, about fifty media conglomerates controlled more than half of all broadcast media, newspapers, magazines, video, radio, music, publishing and film in the country. Today, fewer than ten multinational media conglomerates dominate the American mass media landscape.[28]

A more publicized example of the influence of money and power is how we finance our elections and write our laws. Both the high cost of running for elected office and the enormous amount of resources devoted to lobbying underscore the quantum leap in financial influence that has changed our national politics. In 2000, the average winner of a Senate election spent $7.7 million; the average winner of a House election spent $842,000.[29] Less than 1 percent of the population make contributions of two hundred dollars or more to candidates; half the donors have incomes over $250,000 per year.[30] These contributions clearly have an influence on public policy, particularly on roll call votes on issues that do not attract significant publicity, like special interest tax legislation.[31] And this skewed influence also explains why most senators, while needing to raise over seven thousand dollars a day to run for reelection, don't spend more time at neighborhood diners or soup kitchens. Similarly, the number of paid lobbyists and the scale of contributions to political action committees has spiraled upward for two decades.

Even with campaign finance reform aimed at plugging up some of the avenues of influence, big money will continue to dominate our elections and governing institutions. The result is a government primarily concerned with writing rules and administering regulations to serve the interests of its paying patrons. The power of the political contribution will continue to diminish the power of the ballot. And in the policy contests over the great issues of our day, concentrated wealth will emerge victorious almost all the time.

In this context, the estate tax is a very important issue. The estate tax does make a dent in the dynasties of wealth.[32] If the organized money that is now working to eliminate the tax succeeds, the distribution of wealth and power in our society will become more skewed. The result will be societal rules that are even more beneficial only to those who can pay.

CONCENTRATED WEALTH AND
EQUALITY OF OPPORTUNITY

This concentration of political power directly and indirectly undermines equality of opportunity. The wealthy and powerful generally "privatize" their personal and family needs through private education, private ownership of books and learning tools, private clubs and recreation, private transportation, and so on. For those who are not born wealthy, however, opportunities depend on the existence of strong community and public institutions. The ladder of opportunity for America's middle class depends on strong and accessible public educational institutions, libraries, state parks, and municipal pools. And for America's poor, the ladder of opportunity also includes access to affordable health care, quality public transportation, and child care assistance.

During decades when the concentration of wealth is great, our society puts a greater priority on tax cuts and spending priorities that benefit the wealthy rather than on building the institutions of opportunity.[33] In the 1920s, after several decades of Progressive Era reforms aimed at improving the conditions of ordinary people, there was a widespread rollback of social reforms and public investment. In a similar way, the 1980s and 1990s have witnessed the erosion of investment in equality of opportunity in education, home ownership, and small enterprise development, compared with that of the 1950s and 1960s.

During periods of less wealth inequality, our country has strengthened equality of opportunity, particularly for access to education for people of modest means. This is not only beneficial to the economy but a precondition for electoral democracy. Although our education system has many strong points, we are losing ground in ensuring affordable access for all. In 1965, the Pell grant, the largest federal program for lower-income students, covered 85 percent of the cost of four years at a public university. By 2000, it covered just 39 percent of the cost.

The current political and economic situation, shaped by the priorities of organized wealth, will not improve this picture. College costs have dramatically risen since the late 1970s and will continue to rise. State governments are raising tuition at community colleges and public universities. All of these will be additional obstacles for lower-income students seeking higher education. Those who enroll will endure distracting financial stresses, working long hours while in school and graduating with enormous personal and school debt burdens.

A society with widening disparities of wealth and power chooses other priorities over access to education for all. Historian of U.S. inequality Sam Pizzigati writes that "if we allow great wealth to accumulate in the pockets of a few, then great wealth can set our political agenda and shape our political culture—and the agenda and the culture that emerge will not welcome efforts to make America work for all Americans."[34]

The policy priorities of organized big money are not the same as the priorities of those who are unable to privatize their needs.

GROWING INEQUALITY IS BAD ECONOMIC POLICY
Too much concentrated wealth and power is bad for the economy because it undermines prosperity. Economists have tended to look narrowly at the impact of wealth inequality on economic

efficiency—and they have left it to the worldly philosophers to speculate on the social dangers of concentrated wealth. But a number of economic studies show how too much inequality of income and wealth can be a drag on economic growth. In a survey of academic research on the topic, Philippe Aghion summarizes: "Several studies have examined the impact of inequality upon economic growth. The picture they draw is impressively unambiguous, since they all suggest that greater inequality reduces the rate of growth."[35]

There are several reasons for this pattern. First, as discussed above, countries with high levels of inequality fail to invest adequately in education. Second, as discussed below, inequality leads to a breakdown of social cohesion, and in its most extreme form, to widespread social unrest and political instability.[36] Finally, too much concentrated wealth distorts the investment priorities and market decisions of the country at large, leaving lower- and moderate-income people without the incomes needed to stimulate the economy with widespread consumer spending.

For instance, inequalities of wealth and income backfire in the commercial marketplace. In the last two decades we've seen the emergence of a "Tiffany/Kmart" dichotomy, a two-tier consumer market. One consumer market is shaped to suit the particular tastes and dollars of the top 5 percent of wealth holders. The mass market appeals to the rest. But as the buying power of the middle class erodes, the whole economy is put at risk. The purchasing power of the super wealthy alone is not enough to propel our economy.

After the terrorist attacks and economic downturn of September 2001, several troubling economic trends were unmasked. Commentators expressed concern that the long-term impact of rising consumer debt and stagnant wages might slow our economic recovery. Lower- and middle-income Americans couldn't afford to continue to prime the pump of the U.S. economy with additional consumer borrowing, especially in the face of rising job layoffs. They were maxed out.

Historians have seen this before. In his history of the Depression and Second World War, *Freedom from Fear*, David Kennedy notes how the Hoover administration conducted an extensive survey of social trends on the eve of the Great Depression:

> As Hoover's investigators discovered, the increasing wealth of the 1920s flowed disproportionately to the owners of capital. Worker incomes were rising, but not at a rate that kept pace with the nation's growing industrial output. Without broadly distributed purchasing power, the engines of mass production would have no outlet and would eventually fall idle.[37]

Too much economic inequality undermines economic stability and growth, threatening prosperity for all.

INEQUALITY AND OUR CIVIC AND PUBLIC HEALTH

If too much inequality is bad for our democracy and economy, it is also harmful to the social fabric of a society that aspires toward fairness. British historian Arnold Toynbee analyzed the collapse of twenty-one past civilizations and determined that there were two common factors that led to their demise. The first was a concentration of wealth, and the second was inflexibility in the face of changing conditions.[38] Jeff Gates notes that concentrated wealth and societal rigidity are "two sides of the same coin." Concentrated ownership leads to inflexibility when what societies need is greater cooperation and adaptability.[39]

As our society pulls apart, there is a greater distance between haves and have nots, eroding society's social solidarity and reinforcing a sense that we are in very different realms. Our culture becomes more like an apartheid society, where haves and have nots no longer simply occupy opposite sides of the tracks but inhabit wholly different worlds. And the distance between these worlds has become so wide that it erodes any social sense that we are in this together.

Apartheid societies are unhealthy places to live, for the rich and everyone else. Public health researchers have shown how societies with wide disparities of wealth have poor health. Although it is unhealthy to live in an impoverished community, it is even worse to live in communities with high levels of income and wealth disparities. Within the United States, counties and states with greater inequality, not absolute poverty, have the highest incidences of infant mortality, heart disease, cancer, and homicide. Regions with greater equality enjoy the opposite, longer life expectancies and less violent trauma.[40]

Why is it healthier to live in a community with less inequality? Inequality leads to a breakdown in the social solidarity that is necessary for public health. British medical researcher Richard Wilkerson argues that communities with less inequality have stronger "social cohesion," more cultural limits on unrestrained individual actions, and greater networks of mutual aid and caring. "The individualism and values of the market are restrained by a social morality." The existence of more social capital "lubricates the workings of the whole society and economy. There are fewer signs of antisocial aggressiveness, and society appears more caring."[41]

Nothing demonstrates the fragmentation of community in the United States more vividly than the rise in gated residential communities for the affluent and the simultaneous record numbers of people in prison. Some 9 million households now voluntarily live in gated residential communities and another 2 million people are involuntarily incarcerated.[42] More people than ever are living behind gates and walls with entrances patrolled by armed guards. This polarization disturbs the equilibrium of a democratic society. It is in no one's interest for the United States to become more like some of our South American neighbors, such as Brazil, with such extreme levels of inequality. What kind of nation do we want to become?

The "American experiment" has attempted to balance two competing values: economic liberty versus democracy and equality of opportunity. We want to create a prosperous society, a goal we have achieved for a significant percentage of the population. We also aspire to create a society in which there is equity, where the playing field is level and the runners all start at the same starting line.

As you look over the Forbes 400 list, contemplate what the inevitable multiplication of these large estates will mean for this country in the decades to come. If they are not interrupted by a significant transfer tax, these will become the political dynasties of tomorrow.

There is no possible way for the children, grandchildren, and great-grandchildren of the Forbes 400 to spend the income from these huge estates. Their dynastic wealth will grow and grow, and the accumulation of excessive power in the hands of a limited number poses a significant risk for our society.

DOES THE ESTATE TAX HAVE AN IMPACT?

Some might argue that if one of the goals of the estate tax is to re-duce the concentration of wealth, it is not doing a very good job. After all, the growth in wealth concentration has been enormous and seemingly unchecked by the tax over time. Bruce Bartlett of the libertarian National Center for Policy Analysis observed that "wealth is probably more unequally distributed in the United States than in countries with no estate tax." He compared the mal-distribution of wealth in the United States to four countries—Canada, New Zealand, Australia, and Israel—that don't have an estate tax and have lower levels of wealth inequality. He concludes that since the estate tax is ineffective, it should be scrapped.[43]

Wealth researcher Lisa Keister, however, points out that the wealth distribution in the United States would be much worse without the estate tax. In one simulation, she shows how the dis-tribution of wealth would be different if the estate tax had re-mained as progressive as it was in the mid-1970s, when the top es-tate tax rate was 77 percent and exemptions were lower. Had this rate and exemption structure remained in place during the stock market explosion of the 1990s, it would have greatly reduced wealth inequality. Keister finds that the richest 1 percent would have held just 30 percent of the wealth in 1983, rather than the actual 34 percent of wealth they did possess. And, according to her model, the top 1 percent would have had 32 percent in 1998, rather than the actual 38 percent. The middle class, defined as households between the twentieth and sixtieth percentiles in the distribution, would have had a 10 percent greater share of the wealth pie, rather than losing ground.[44]

In another scenario, Keister demonstrates that the concentration of wealth would have been much greater if the progressivity of the estate tax had been reduced. Under this scenario, the top 1 percent would have owned 37 percent of the nation's wealth in 1983 and 43 percent in 1998. Remember, the actual figures are that the top 1 percent owned 34 percent of the nation's wealth in 1983 and 38 percent in 1998.[45]

It is clear that the 2001 reforms of the estate tax will increase wealth inequality—and that complete repeal will further fuel greater concentrations of wealth. Indeed, the estate tax could be more effective in deterring wealth imbalances. We should strengthen the tax, not eliminate it.

CHAPTER TWO

The Origins of America's Estate Tax

> They will put up with poverty, servitude, and barbarism, but they
> will not endure aristocracy.
>   —Alexis de Tocqueville[1]

One May morning in 2001, during our effort to preserve the estate tax, the authors sat down with the editorial board of a distinguished major newspaper. After orange juice and pleasantries, the
editors began to pepper us with questions that had become familiar to us over the preceding months. What about the impact of the
estate tax on small business owners? Isn't it immoral to have a tax
on people at death? Don't you think the estate tax is fundamentally un-American?

We offered our perspective on these and other common questions. But our question for them, as gatekeepers of the public
discourse, concerned the absence of a larger public conversation.
Shouldn't we, as a society, have a more rigorous discussion about
the dangers of concentrated wealth and power at this time? Does
our society have any interest or responsibility to limit the great
fortunes in our midst?

Our national identity was forged, as we expelled the British
monarchy, in our rejection of hereditary political and economic
power. Our nation's founders believed that our success as a republic was conditioned upon limiting disparities of wealth. For our
first 150 years as a republic, our leaders understood that there was a
troubling nexus between accumulated economic power and concentrated political power. So while our nation held closely to the
values of economic liberty and free enterprise, it remained vigi-

lant to ensure that our fragile self-governing society would not succumb to the corrupting influences of consolidated wealth and power.

Yet as the Industrial Revolution turned the pioneer farmer into a factory worker, the excesses of the Gilded Age called for new mechanisms to protect our economic and political vitality. The shocking economic disparities of this age moved the nation to act because we realized that our society was becoming like the European systems that we had rejected.

One hundred years ago our country had a vibrant debate—in the public square and in Congress—about the great disparities of wealth and power that existed at that time. This robust controversy over how to address these inequalities involved ordinary men and women and the elites of that time, the Carnegies, Rockefellers, and Roosevelts. The debate coursed among farmers, urban reformers, religious leaders, and nascent labor unions. It ran in the newspapers and media of the day, including muckrakers and staid opinion journals like the *North American Review.*

Many 1900–1918 Progressive Era reforms resulted from this period, such as child labor laws, direct election of U.S. senators, and the establishment of an income tax, which required the extraordinary step of amending the Constitution. The estate tax was one of these reforms. Like the income tax, it was a fundamentally American response, rooted in our republican heritage, to the belief that great aggregations of wealth were dangerous to our democracy and civic health. There was also a recognition that great wealth should pay a greater portion of public needs. Let's examine in detail how the estate tax got started.

AMERICAN VALUES: THE ROOTS OF THE ESTATE TAX
The essence of the American experiment is our collective rejection of European hereditary aristocracy and grotesque inequalities of wealth. When Alexis de Tocqueville visited the United States in the mid-nineteenth century, he noted that equality of condition permeated the American spirit: "The American experiment presupposes a rejection of inherited privilege." In the words of

novelist John Dos Passos, "rejection of Europe is what America is all about."[2]

The nation's founders and populace viewed excessive concentrations of wealth as incompatible with the ideals of the new nation. Revolutionary era visitors to Europe, including Thomas Jefferson, John Adams, and Ben Franklin, were aghast at the wide disparities of wealth and poverty they observed. They surmised that these great European inequalities were the result of an aristocratic system of land transfers, hereditary political power, and monopoly.[3]

Monarchies and hereditary aristocracies mocked the republican principle of self-government. Writing in *Common Sense*, Thomas Paine attacked the notion of hereditary government. "To the evil of monarchy we have added that of hereditary succession; and as the first is a degradation and lessening of ourselves, so the second, claimed as a matter of right, is an insult and imposition on posterity."[4]

In two other articles, "Rights of Man" and "Agrarian Justice," Paine extended his contempt of inherited political power to a critique of inherited economic power. Paine proposed an inheritance tax that would fund an early version of Social Security.[5]

The distrust of concentrated wealth was so great that, in an extreme sentiment, Ben Franklin argued "that no man ought to own more property than needed for his livelihood; the rest, by right, belonged to the state."[6] One could not accumulate vast wealth, in the republican worldview, simply through one's own labors. In small-scale agrarian freeholder society, where land ownership was more widely distributed among men of European ancestry, there was a "natural distribution of wealth." Farmers, artisans, and other workers reaped the "fruits of their own labor."

In 1776, artisans from Philadelphia put forward a provision for inclusion in the original state constitution of Pennsylvania. They advocated for a limit on the concentration of wealth. "An enormous Proportion of Property vested in a few Individuals is dangerous to the Rights, and destructive of the Common Happiness of Mankind; and therefore any free State hath a Right by its Laws to discourage the Possession of such Property."[7]

The provision was narrowly rejected. But the concern about inequality and accumulated wealth was present at the formation of our nation.

Indeed, central to American republicanism was the principle of a broad and fair distribution of wealth and property. Noah Webster, writing in favor of adopting the U.S. Constitution in 1787, expressed that "a general and tolerably equal distribution of landed property is the whole basis of national freedom" and widespread distribution of property was "the very soul of a republic."[8] Too much inequality was a threat to a self-governing society. Without an equitable land distribution, the founders believed, the republic would not survive.

John Adams also viewed broad land ownership as a key ingredient in maintaining a balance of political power. He was greatly influenced by seventeenth-century philosopher James Harrington, who argued that the widespread distribution of property dispersed power.[9] Adams believed that when "economic power became concentrated in a few hands, then political power flowed to those possessors and away from the citizens, ultimately resulting in an oligarchy or tyranny."[10] In a 1776 letter to James Sullivan, Adams articulated his perspective that a balance in property ownership was essential to liberty.

> The balance of power in a society, accompanies the balance of property in land. The only possible way, then, of preserving the balance of power on the side of equal liberty and public virtue, is to make the acquisition of land easy to every member of society; to make a division of land into small quantities, so that the multitude may be possessed of landed estates. If the multitude is possessed of the balance of real estate, the multitude will take care of the liberty, virtue, and interest of the multitude, in all acts of government.[11]

Thomas Jefferson, writing to James Madison in 1785, made the now famous statement that "the small land holders are the most precious part of a state." He argued that legislators could not invent too many devices for subdividing property, "only taking care to let their subdivisions go hand in hand with the natural affections of the human mind."[12]

In the republican worldview, European aristocrats created unbalanced distributions of wealth by controlling the land through inheritance laws of primogeniture and entail. These land tenure systems allowed land transfers only to oldest male children, maintaining hereditary concentrations of land rather than broadly distributing it. In a conscious rejection of primogeniture, Jefferson wrote,

> The descent of property of every kind therefore to all children, or to all the brothers and sisters, or other relations in equal degree, is a politic measure, and a practicable one. Another means of silently lessening the inequality of property is to exempt all from taxation below a certain point, and to tax the higher portions of property in geometrical progression as they rise.[13]

The revolutionaries believed in *equitability*, a notion of relative equality and fairness, rather than rigid equality. Revolutionary writers and orators underscored that American society would have modest inequalities. "The utopian schemes of leveling, and a community of goods," wrote Sam Adams, "are as visionary and impracticable, as those which vest all property in the Crown." Rigid equality, according to Sam Adams, would be "arbitrary, despotic, and in our government unconstitutional." Minor inequalities would exist as the result of differences in individual talent, effort, and modest variations in property ownership.[14]

This equitability translated into a culture that was antiaristocratic in sentiment. To be labeled an aristocrat or to be accused of advocating for "aristocratic policies" was the ultimate political slander in revolutionary America. For instance, John Adams through much of his later years had to fight the whispers that he had "monarchist sympathies," having spent so many years consorting with royalty in France and England.[15]

The founders celebrated the exceptionalism of the American

experiment and heartily rejected aristocratic politics and economic policy. "The economic agenda for a republic became clear," writes James Huston. "Enact the opposite of aristocratic legislation."[16]

What made the new nation unique was its relative equality. Noah Webster exuded confidence in the justness of the American system: "Here the equalizing genius of the laws distributes property to every citizen."[17] In other words, no rent to an absentee landlord or land ownership monopolies.

In their enthusiasm, the revolutionaries glossed over some of the enormous inequalities that existed in colonial society, the most obvious of which was the existence of slavery.[18] "American society was not egalitarian and some individuals possessed impressive amounts of wealth," writes Huston. "An elite did exist, and much of its property had come from political favoritism, inheritance, or family connections."[19] At the same time, their prescriptions for addressing this inequality were overly simplistic. For instance, the founders thought that eliminating the aristocratic land laws of entails and primogeniture would institutionalize relative equality. John Adams and Thomas Jefferson wrote confidently that America's land tenure system encouraged subdivision and a broader distribution of land ownership, preventing aristocratic concentrations of ownership.[20] Our nation's founders were blind to some of the inequalities in their midst. But our national creed—with its aspiration to greater equality and suspicion of accumulated wealth and power—was forged at the time of our nation's independence.

Economic historians have caricatured American economic thought as a conflict between Jeffersonian democratic egalitarians and Hamiltonian free market capitalists. But as historian Joseph J. Ellis observed, "the projection of their debate as the archetypal dialogue in American political culture has become a historical cartoon."[21] In reality, both of these "founding brothers" shared a concern for balancing an unjust concentration of political power with liberty and free enterprise. Hamilton was more enamored with concentrations of economic power because they represented capital, or the "synergy of aggregated investment." Yet both Hamilton and Jefferson shared a rejection of the aristocratic economic system that allowed a few people to appropriate the fruits of labor of others, resulting in an unjust accumulation of property and wealth.[22] The revolution never resolved this tension between economic freedom and democracy; rather it "contained the explosive energies of that debate within an ongoing argument that was eventually institutionalized in political parties and built into the fabric of our national identity." This balancing act lived within the republican consensus, a worldview that was to last almost 125 years.[23]

THE GILDED AGE AND THE MOVEMENT
FOR AN ESTATE TAX

The push for a permanent estate tax came as a result of the inequalities brought about by the Industrial Revolution and the excesses of the Gilded Age. These changes shattered American's self-perception, reflected in De Toqueville's observations, of ourselves as an egalitarian society. Although great inequalities existed and accelerated during the nineteenth century, it was around 1880 that a widely shared perception emerged that the nation had gone adrift from its republican moorings.

Investigative journalism, social protest movements, and academic studies combined to dramatize that America now had unacceptable concentrations of wealth and power. James Huston notes that prior to 1886 there was a paucity of written material about inequality, but after that year "the periodical press erupted with articles devoted solely to the question of wealth distribution. Unlike earlier years, when discussion of American wealth distribution was usually a signal for self-congratulation, the articles and speeches appearing in the 1880s and 1890s were lamentations."[24]

Among the factors that shook the republican worldview was documentation of the country's concentration of land ownership and poverty, land being the primary form of wealth holding. In 1879, Henry George published *Progress and Poverty*, a book chronicling the dangers of consolidated land ownership. This remarkable book, which would today be considered too dense to enjoy a wide readership, sold over 1 million copies, and excerpts were serialized in several popular magazines.[25]

Another factor shaking republican ideals was the dramatic expansion of the nation's industrial capacity in the form of the large-scale business corporation. The pace of corporate consolidation at this time was breathtaking. In the merger wave of 1897 to 1904, some 4,227 firms consolidated into 257 companies. Massive combinations in banking, industry, and railroads led to cries of "monopoly" and antitrust intervention.[26] Mass production and monopoly, which had been slowly emerging over the previous several decades, began to touch more people's lives. James Huston noted that "in a wave of pools, trusts, and then mergers, large business enterprise took over the core production of the American economy. That change induced a panic mentality among commentators who feared that now the distribution of wealth was becoming permanently warped and unsuitable for republican institutions."[27]

After centuries of small-scale enterprise, many people found the economy dominated by massive trusts in railroads, sugar, oil, and other necessities essential to every household.[28] At the same time, the opulent wealth of the Gilded Age was staggering, especially in contrast to the impoverished urban workforce. The mansions of Newport were constructed against a backdrop of largely immigrant workers crowding into the unsanitary tenements of the new industrial era. This disparity, combined with widespread political corruption, fueled a backlash against dynastic wealth.[29]

A number of social protest movements emerged between 1870 and 1910 including agrarian populism, the early labor union effort, and the religious Social Gospel movement. Protests about the trusts, political corruption, and unequal wealth were so widespread that by 1890 the national political platforms of all three major parties harshly condemned economic concentration.

The movement that pressed for establishment of a permanent estate tax was varied, including rural populists and urban progressives. In many respects, the rural populist movement of the 1880s and 1890s was the most broad-based social movement in American history.[30] Agrarian reformers in the South and West established over two hundred independent newspapers, and hundreds of orators traveled the rural byways, forming the base of the insurgent Populist Party.

The Populist Party platform in 1888 called for the establishment of an income tax, direct election of U.S. senators, and aggressive enforcement of antitrust laws. The populists agitated against the railroad trusts as the midwives of the monopoly. Presidential candidate William Jennings Bryan sought the presidency three times, campaigning on a platform that included establishing an income tax. Although he lost each of his bids, the movement behind his candidacies changed the country's political landscape.

Part of this movement was organized labor. Between 1884 and 1886, membership in the Knights of Labor increased from 71,000 to over 700,000.[31] The Knights of Labor were alarmed at the emerging inequality of wealth and proposed worker ownership of enterprises as a solution to broaden wealth ownership and lessen inequality of outcome.

In 1886 and 1887, the number of labor strikes dramatically increased.[32] During the 1892 Homestead strike at Carnegie Steel Works near Pittsburgh, Pinkerton security forces were ordered to fire at workers and their families. Ron Chernow observed:

> Such corporate truculence provoked calls by the new Populist Party for a graduated income tax, government ownership of railroad and telegraph companies, and tougher safeguards for trade unions. As the country grew more polarized, many people wondered whether America had paid too dear a price for the industrialization that had so quickly propelled it from an agrarian society to a world economic power.[33]

Between 1898 and 1905, the total membership in American trade unions went from seven hundred thousand to 2 million. By 1917, the ranks of labor membership had grown to 3 million.[34]

A new generation of investigative and muckraker journalists engaged in the "literature of exposure," including Ida Tarbel's expose of Standard Oil, Lincoln Steffens's profiles of urban corruption, and Henry Demarest Lloyd's tome about the abuses of the large trusts.[35] A utopian novel depicting an egalitarian society, *Looking Backward,* by Edward Bellamy, was published in 1888 and became one of the best-selling books of the century, third only to the Bible and *Ben Hur. Looking Backward* inspired the formation of hundreds of Bellamy societies and "Nationalist Clubs" that convened to popularize the credo of the book and agitate for a more egalitarian society.

In the arena of religion, the Social Gospel movement was making connections between biblical teachings and social conditions of the country. Protestant evangelicals deplored the moral crisis that accompanied industrialization and the lopsided distribution of wealth.[36]

In 1891, Pope Leo XIII wrote one of the first Catholic Social Encyclicals, *Rerum Novarum* (On the Condition of Workers), with encouragement from American Catholic leaders. In a departure from previous religious social teachings ascribing virtue to great wealth and encouraging acceptance of oppressive conditions among the working class, *Rerum Novarum* recognized the inherent dignity of all work and the rights of workers.[37]

At the turn of the century, upheaval and inequality encouraged in many people an apocalyptic outlook on the prospects for democracy. Eltweed Pomeroy, the author of an 1896 study of wealth disparity in Massachusetts, sounded the alarm with his inquiry: "Can this [concentration of wealth] continue and the Republic live? No; either the propertyless masses will rise in bloody revolution and snatch from the wealth some part of their 'ill-gotten gains' or the country would endure the worst 'despotism of wealth' the world had ever seen."[38]

These social movements made the establishment of income and inheritance taxes a central part of their political program. Sidney Ratner noted that this "inheritance tax movement which had existed before the Civil War in various states had undergone a resurgence in the late eighteen–eighties and nineties."[39] They worked initially at the state level, where the New York State inheritance tax law of 1892 became a model for other states. Between 1890 and 1900, eighteen states passed inheritance taxes, some with progressive rates.[40]

EARLY ESTATE TAXATION

Prior to 1913, the ultimate rationale for implementing national inheritance taxes was the need for revenue during times of war. The first federal tax on wealth was levied in 1797, when the United States was faced with the escalating costs of responding to French attacks on American shipping. Congress imposed a stamp duty on receipts for legacies and probates for wills. The tax was eliminated in 1802 as the conflict ended.

During the nineteenth century, federal government revenue came primarily from excise taxes and tariffs. Income and estate taxes were imposed only during revenue emergencies resulting from the Civil War and the Spanish-American Wars. Wartime taxation, or the "conscription of wealth" as it was called by its advocates, was perceived as equitable because of the unequal sacrifice of different citizens. At a time when some men and women sacrificed their lives, sometimes as soldier proxies for wealthier citizens, taxation of wealth seemed a just levy for the war effort. As was to be the case throughout the nineteenth century, these wartime taxes were repealed once the war concluded or wartime debts were paid.[41]

A federal inheritance tax on beneficiaries was passed as part of the Tax Act of 1862 and helped pay for the Civil War. This tax was reenacted and codified in the Internal Revenue Law of 1864. It contained many features of subsequent estate tax laws, such as deductions for charitable bequests, special treatment for bequests to surviving spouses, and exemptions of small estates. It was repealed in 1870 as war debts were paid off.

In 1894 Congress passed an income tax, but it was struck down as unconstitutional by the U.S. Supreme Court on the grounds that it inappropriately discriminated among residents of different states. Proponents had to wait another generation for the introduction of the Sixteenth Amendment to the U.S. Constitution in 1913 and the ratification of two-thirds of U.S. states.

The inheritance tax, however, faced no constitutional problems as it was considered an excise tax at death rather than an income tax. The number of states with an inheritance tax continued to increase, primarily in the eastern United States. A federal inheritance tax did make a brief appearance, however, at the century's end. In order to generate revenue for the Spanish-American War, Congress passed the War Revenue Act of 1898. Instead of a tax on beneficiaries of inheritance, this act imposed a tax on estates, a precursor to our contemporary estate tax system. The tax was repealed in 1902 at the termination of hostilities.

Over the thirty years between 1880 and 1910, proposals for permanent federal income and estate taxes were blocked by conservative forces in Congress. Meanwhile, the concentrations of wealth and power became more visible and troubling, leading to a wide array of powerful supporters for a tax on wealth.

SUPPORTERS OF THE ESTATE TAX

The growth of income and wealth disparities, and the resulting social movements, changed the nature of American politics at the beginning of the twentieth century. Even our homegrown industrial titans shared sentiments for change, an early appearance of a movement for wealth and responsibility.

Andrew Carnegie was among the most articulate voices on the dangers of inequality. When the Scottish-born industrialist sold his steelworks to John Pierpont Morgan Sr. for $480 million in 1901 ($8.5 billion in 2002 dollars), Carnegie had amassed the biggest fortune in American history. According to one estimate, his total accumulated wealth was equal to one-half of the nation's annual gross national product at the time.[42]

Carnegie did not advocate tampering with the wealth-creating machinery. He believed that enforcing equality of economic outcomes in production was a hopeless task. But he was concerned about the inequalities that resulted from the same industrial economic system that generated fabulous amounts of wealth. The innovation of utilizing a division of labor in production, Carnegie observed, served as a powerful force for competition, achievement, and progress, yet it also had the side effect of producing great disparities.

Carnegie argued that "we must accommodate ourselves [to] great inequality of environment; the concentration of business, industrial and commercial, in the hands of a few." This was not only beneficial "but essential to the future progress of the race." Industrial owners "under the free play of economic forces, of necessity, soon will be in receipt of more revenue than can be judiciously expended upon themselves."[43]

Carnegie was troubled by the polarization of the Gilded Age and advocated a two-part program to address it. The first part of Carnegie's program was the imposition of stiff income and inheritance taxes to pay for the second part of his program, the redistribution of wealth through charity and government action.

Carnegie testified before Congress in support of a large inheritance tax. He believed that the tax would discourage the wealthy from having undue advantages and would encourage charitable giving during a person's lifetime, rather than wealth accumulation. Carnegie celebrated the trend toward income and estate taxes. At a time when his home state of Pennsylvania taxed one-tenth of property at death and England was increasing inheritance taxes, Carnegie approvingly observed, "the growing disposition to tax more and more heavily large estates left at death is a cheering indication of the growth of a salutary change in public opinion."[44] On the matter of estate taxes, Carnegie said,

> Of all forms of taxation this seems the wisest. Men who continue hoarding great sums all their lives, the proper use of which for public ends would work good to the community from which it chiefly came, should be made to feel that the community, in the form of the State, cannot thus be deprived of its proper share. By taxing estates heavily at death the State marks its condemnation of the selfish millionaire's unworthy life.[45]

In *The Gospel of Wealth,* Carnegie articulated his view of radical meritocracy. He believed that each generation should "have to start anew with equal opportunities. Their struggle to achieve would, generation after generation, bring the best and the brightest to the top." According to historian Peter Dobkin Hall, Carnegie thought that "each individual would be allowed to find his place—and his just rewards—in the industrial hierarchy, each according to his ability. But the attainment of that place [should give] neither advantages nor handicaps to his children."[46]

The second pillar of Carnegie's program for addressing inequality was the creation of a strong infrastructure of public and private institutions to ensure equality of opportunity. Although his charitable actions are often cited as a "paean to private philanthropy," he gave enormous amounts of money to public institutions as well, such as public education, libraries, parks, bathhouses, and other facilities.[47]

Not everyone was supportive of broadening income and wealth taxation. In the first decade of the new century, the wealth of John D. Rockefeller began to surpass even that of Andrew Carnegie. Rockefeller, however, was opposed to taxation. In a 1914 interview he stated that "when a man has accumulated a sum of money, accumulated it within the law, the Government has no right to share in its earnings."[48]

Still, Rockefeller shared the fundamental American distaste for the trappings of European aristocracy. Speaking in admiration of Napoleon, Rockefeller noted that "he was a human being and virile because he came direct from the ranks of the people. There was none of the stagnant blood of nobility or royalty in his veins."[49]

With the establishment of the Rockefeller Foundation in 1913, a tremendous amount of that family fortune was insulated from taxation. And as the Sixteenth Amendment passed and estate taxes were instituted, biographer Ron Chernow speculated as to the uniqueness of Rockefeller's situation:

> As taxes became steeper and more progressive in the coming decades,
> it became a daunting task for any businessman to amass the money

that Rockefeller had earned in a laissez-faire world devoid of anti-trust laws. His own wealth, in fact, was the text for many sermons in favor of using taxation as a way to check the acquisition of huge fortunes, to redistribute wealth, and to reduce social tensions.[50]

As president, patrician Theodore Roosevelt took up the unlikely mantle of trust-buster and advocate of progressive taxation. Roosevelt saw his role as preserving the capitalist system by steering a course between socialist demands and the excesses of corporate power and organized wealth. In his celebrated speech of April 1906, he attacked both the "muckrakers," a term he coined, and the privileged classes. He championed

> the adoption of some such scheme as that of the progressive tax on all fortunes, beyond a certain amount either given in life or devised or bequeathed upon death to any individual—a tax so framed as to put it out of the power of the owner of one of these enormous fortunes to hand on more than a certain amount to any one individual; the tax, of course, to be imposed by the National and not the State Government. Such taxation should, of course, be aimed merely at the inheritance or transmission in their entirety of those fortunes swollen beyond all healthy limits.[51]

In December 1906, President Roosevelt spoke out in favor of the estate tax, saying its "primary objective should be to put a constantly increasing burden on the inheritance of those swollen fortunes which it is certainly of no benefit to this country to perpetuate."[52] A year later, Roosevelt intoned against the "malefactors of great wealth" and became an outspoken advocate for the Sixteenth Amendment to institute an income tax. In a June 1907 speech, he told the American people that "most great civilized countries have an income tax and an inheritance tax. In my judgement both should be part of our system of federal taxation."[53]

One of Roosevelt's appointments to the Supreme Court was Massachusetts jurist Oliver Wendell Holmes. Holmes is well known for his statement, now engraved on the IRS's headquarters, that "taxes are the price we pay for civilization." Upon his own death, Holmes bequeathed the bulk of his estate to the federal government.[54]

After Theodore Roosevelt retired to private life, President William Howard Taft continued his predecessor's advocacy for both a federal inheritance tax and a constitutional amendment to allow an income tax. Though President Taft was conservative and disinclined toward progressive taxation, he was caught up in the national groundswell in opposition to expanding the tariff. Progressive Republicans led the way toward including an inheritance tax in the 1909 Tariff Bill, a provision drafted by Representative Cordell Hull of Tennessee. It was blocked in the Senate by powerful Republican old-guard members led by Rhode Island senator Nelson Aldrich.[55]

In the summer of 1910, private citizen Theodore Roosevelt returned from a world tour and began a national speaking tour in favor of what he called the "New Nationalism." His speeches were inspired by Herbert Croly's groundbreaking book, *The Promise of American Life,* which called for strong government intervention to strengthen democracy and foster social justice. Sidney Ratner observed that "Roosevelt stressed the need for advanced social legislation, attacked reactionary decisions of the Supreme Court, and advocated changing the rules of the economic game so as to bring about greater equality of opportunity and reward."[56] Progressive Republican leaders rallied to Roosevelt's call and led the fight for the estate and income tax system.

THE ESTABLISHMENT OF THE ESTATE TAX

Early in the twentieth century, Gilded Age corruption and inequality, powerful and popular social movements, and growing moral misgivings within the wealthy elite all converged on America's political stage. Out of that convergence came America's first lasting estate tax. Those who made the case for that estate tax advanced arguments that have all but vanished from the contemporary debate.

First was the belief that the hereditary transfer of concentrated wealth was incompatible with professed American values and democratic aspirations. Several decades after the passage of the tax, Franklin D. Roosevelt rearticulated these American sentiments when he affirmed the importance of building wealth and warned of the dangers of its overconcentration. "The desire to provide security for one's self and one's family is natural and wholesome," FDR argued, and "it is adequately served by a reasonable inheritance." But enormous inheritances should be scrutinized.

> Great accumulations of wealth cannot be justified on the basis of personal and family security. . . . In the last analysis, such accumulations [of inherited wealth] amount to the perpetuation of great and undesirable concentration of control in a relatively few individuals. . . . Such inherited economic power is as inconsistent with the ideals of this generation as inherited political power was inconsistent with the ideals of the generation which established our government.[57]

A second belief was that society played a significant role in the creation of individual wealth and therefore had some claim upon the wealth of the very rich. This was explicit in President Theodore Roosevelt's message to Congress when he proposed a federal inheritance tax on December 4, 1906. "The man of great wealth owes a particular obligation to the State because he derives special advantages from the mere existence of government." In a paraphrase of Adam Smith, Roosevelt added, "It is only under the shelter of the civil magistrate that the owner of valuable property can sleep a single night in security." Roosevelt and others of his day recognized that wealthy citizens got a good deal from government, not least being the protection of wealth and property rights.

The push for a permanent inheritance tax gained a lot of ground in the years leading up to 1916. The number of states with inheritance taxes increased from twenty-six in 1902 to forty-two in 1916.[58] And President Woodrow Wilson was swept into office in 1912 by a reform movement with an agenda that included ratification of the Income Tax Amendment in 1913 and the establishment of an inheritance tax. This same election swept aside some of the old guard of the Senate, who had blocked social legislation and progressive tax proposals. The permanent estate tax, after a generation of agitation, got a final push toward passage as part of war preparations and was included in the Emergency Revenue Act of 1916. The 1916 act also increased income taxes and instituted an excess profits tax to discourage war profiteering.

In addition to wartime revenue needs, the political impetus for the 1916 Emergency Revenue Act was to reduce the amount of federal revenue derived from customs and excise taxes, viewed by many to be regressive because they fell harder on farm states and wage earners. In the words of one legislator, the tariff was a license to "rob and plunder industrious consumers."[59] In 1916, individual and corporate income taxes accounted for only 16 percent of federal revenues; the balance of revenue came from tariffs and excise taxes.

The shift from excise taxes and tariffs to income and estate taxes reflected a realignment of geographical political power within the United States. Proponents of the income and estate tax came from the South, Midwest, and West, agrarian regions whose voters had low incomes and little wealth but suffered disproportionately from the excise tax and tariffs. Opposition to income and estate taxation came from the Northeast, which had a disproportionate share of income and wealth.

During the 1916 debate over whether to expand the income tax and institute an estate tax, the House Ways and Means Committee report urged that revenue should be levied upon "the incomes and inheritances of those deriving the most benefit from government." Not everyone was pleased, however. Ohio congressman Nicholas Longworth, the son-in-law of President Theodore Roosevelt, criticized the package as "class legislation," objecting to the way it singled out the wealthy for taxation.[60] But Representative Cordell Hull turned this notion on its head, noting that the protective tariff was part of an "infamous system of class legislation" that imposed a major burden on the American people while "virtually exempting the Carnegies, the Vanderbilts, the Morgans, and the Rockefellers, with aggregated billions of hoarded wealth."[61] Hull, who went on to serve in the Senate and then as secretary of state under FDR, summed up the difference between opposing politicians: "An irrepressible conflict has been raging for a thousand years between the strong and the weak, and the former always trying to heap the chief tax burdens upon the latter. That conflict still continues."[62]

The first estate tax was imposed on the value of an estate over fifty thousand dollars (roughly $350,000 in 2002 dollars) at a graduated rate of 1 to 5 percent. This easily excluded the vast majority of the population. Although most of the costs associated with the First World War were financed through bonds, there was tremendous pressure to raise new revenue through taxation. Within six months of the estate tax's passage, Congress raised the rates, concerned that the excess profits tax it had passed would prove difficult to administer and would not generate sufficient revenue. The revised bill was signed by President Woodrow Wilson, but it never went into effect as the United States entered into war on April 5, 1917.

The need for more wartime revenue finally led to the passage of the 1917 War Revenue Act with large bipartisan majorities. In the climate of the First World War, the rallying cries of "ability to pay" and "war profiteering" drowned out concerns of "class legislation." Wartime estate tax rates were increased to a low of 2 percent on taxable estates under fifty thousand dollars up to a high 25 percent on estates exceeding $10 million (the equivalent of over $140 million today).[63] Tax legislation passed during the war fell largely on the very wealthy. In 1920, only 5.5 million income tax returns were filed for a population of 106 million and a labor force of over 41 million.[64]

The establishment of income and estate taxes was a victory, after almost two generations of advocacy, primarily in rural states. The First World War virtually ended the importance of the tariff as a source of revenue and greatly diminished the role of excise taxes. During the war years of 1917 to 1918, income taxes grew to account for almost 59 percent of federal revenue. The wartime taxes also represented a significant shift in the tax burden onto those most able to pay. An estimated 74 percent of the revenue generated by the War Revenue Act of 1917 came from new taxes on the wealthy, including the income tax, the estate tax, and the excess profits tax. By comparison, 13 percent came from consumption taxes and 13 percent from other forms of taxation.[65]

In the two decades after 1917, the estate tax structure underwent many changes, including adjustments to the rate structure and exemption threshold, institution of gift taxes to discourage income and estate tax avoidance, and expansion of some deductions. The contemporary concerns about liquidity for small business were addressed as well.

After the First World War, there was a general call for a "return to normalcy," including the dismantling of war taxes. This coincided with the beginning of Andrew Mellon's powerful tenure as secretary of the treasury and his strong advocacy for reduced taxes. Historians have observed that "three presidents served under Andrew Mellon."

During the 1920s, Mellon led an incremental reduction of corporate and individual taxes. He articulated arguments about the need for capital formation and reduced taxation that would make today's devotees of "supply-side" economics proud. Yet he also made a strong distinction between "earned" and "unearned income," money coming from wages compared with income from investments. Mellon believed that the latter should shoulder greater tax burdens. Contemporary tax debates would benefit from Mellon's insight, as the trend in recent decades has been to shift the tax burden off of unearned income, such as capital gains, and onto earned income, such as wages. Yet Mellon advocated the opposite:

> The fairness of taxing more lightly incomes from wages, salaries or from investments is beyond question. In the first case, the income is uncertain and limited in duration; sickness or death destroys it and old age diminishes it; in the other, the source of income continues; the income may be disposed of during a man's life and it descends to his heirs.
>
> Surely we can afford to make a distinction between the people whose only capital is their mental and physical energy and the people

whose income is derived from investments. Such a distinction would mean much to millions of American workers and would be an added inspiration to the man who must provide a competence during his few productive years to care for himself and his family when his earnings capacity is at an end.[66]

Mellon was practical about the estate tax, eventually lobbying for increased rates during the Great Depression as a means to balance the budget. Many of that day understood that elimination of the federal estate tax would shift tax burdens off of those with wealth and onto those whose income, in Mellon's words, was "uncertain and limited in duration."

During the 1920s, the estate tax was actively debated and amended. While the United States reduced estate taxes, France, England, and other European countries were moving in the opposite direction, imposing steeper inheritance taxes. Successful businessman Harlan E. Read argued in his book *The Abolition of Inheritance* that war debts should be paid off with heavy taxes on inherited wealth.[67]

Progressive Republicans and Democrats were concerned that people were evading the estate tax by transferring property as gifts to heirs prior to death. One beneficiary of the absence of a gift tax was the Rockefeller family. John D. Rockefeller transferred an estimated $475 million of his fortune to his heirs between 1917 and 1922, the equivalent of over $4 billion today. By the time the gift tax was instituted, Rockefeller owned less than $20 million to $25 million in his own name.[68] In 1924, Congress instituted a gift tax to close a loophole that enabled wealthy donors to give unlimited gifts to heirs to altogether avoid income and estate taxation. But two years later, after "the high pressure politics of the propertied classes," the gift tax was repealed, reopening the significant loophole.[69]

During the revenue debates of 1926, Secretary Mellon and President Coolidge's administration worked to institute the major tax reductions they had campaigned for. They proposed complete abolition of estate and gift taxes along with an ample package of income and corporate tax reductions. Historian Sidney Ratner writes that a "vast propaganda machine" was deployed "with the aid of numerous financiers and industrialists" to sell the public and Congress on the Mellon tax plan.[70] Mellon and Coolidge won most of what they asked for. But while the Senate voted to completely repeal the estate tax, the House passed a compromise that reduced estate tax rates by 50 percent and increased the credit allowed for payment of state inheritance taxes from 25 to 80 percent. This credit was significant, as inheritance taxes in some states were higher than federal estate taxes. Raising the credit greatly reduced federal estate tax revenue.

The Revenue Act of 1928, the fourth straight tax reduction of the 1920s, focused on reducing taxes on corporations. The estate tax rates were kept at their 1926 levels, but not without a fight. An exasperated William R. Green, chairman of the House Ways and Means Committee, characterized the estate tax repeal effort as "the most extraordinary, highly financed propaganda for a selfish purpose . . . that has ever been known in the whole history of the country."[71]

During the Depression years, these changes in the estate tax were reversed. In 1932, President Hoover and Secretary Mellon worked to balance the budget with the Revenue Act of 1932. Secretary Mellon, responding to a growing fiscal crisis, testified in favor of tax increases and proposed a rollback of the major tax reductions that he had orchestrated in 1926 and 1928. Estate tax rates were doubled from their 1926 level and the gift tax was reinstated.[72] In 1934, estate and gift tax rates were increased again.

By the mid-1930s, the polarization of income and wealth became an even more acute political issue. In June 1935, President Roosevelt sent remarks to Congress in which he criticized the revenue system for having "done little to prevent an unjust concentration of wealth and economic power."[73] In one speech he denounced the aggressive tax avoidance of some of the country's wealthier families, including one family's creation of 197 separate family trusts to reduce taxation.[74]

Roosevelt rearticulated many of the reasons for an estate tax, including the perspective that society plays a significant role in the creation of wealth and that too much concentrated wealth undermines the common good.

> Wealth in the modern world resulted from a combination of individual efforts. In spite of the great importance in our national life of the . . . ingenuity of unusual individuals, the people in the mass have inevitably helped to make large fortunes possible. The transmission of these fortunes from generation to generation was not consistent with American ideals. Accumulation of wealth, moreover, perpetuated great and undesirable concentration of control in a relatively few individuals over the employment and welfare of many, many others.[75]

FDR proposed an inheritance tax to go along with the existing estate tax, the proceeds of which would go toward retirement of the national debt. But he had private concerns about the inheritance tax and did not push it vigorously.[76] Instead, Congress increased existing estate and gift taxes significantly. Of note was the highly graduated rate on the largest fortunes, including a 70 percent levy on the amount of fortunes in excess of $50 million.[77]

Between 1942 and 1976, the fundamental structure of the estate tax remained largely unchanged. President Truman was a proponent of increasing the estate tax, but he was unable to prevail in a conservative Congress. A few provisions were clarified or added, including the deduction for bequests to spouses and the expansion of taxable assets to include life insurance. In 1958, a ten-year payment period for estates with small business assets was added.

During the early 1960s, President Kennedy proposed a significant change to how capital gains were assessed, from a "stepped-up" basis to a "carryover" basis at death.[78] The difference between stepped-up and carryover applies to unrealized capital gains on assets that are bequeathed at death. They frequently escape taxation and instead the cost or basis of these assets is either arbitrarily stepped up to their market value at the time of death or carried over.

For example, Aunt Milly acquires a valuable painting for $10,000. Forty years later, upon her death, the painting is bequeathed to her niece Margaret. Under the stepping-up scheme, the value of the painting is now appraised at $110,000. The $100,000 capital gain is not taxed and the cost of the painting is stepped up—increased to its current value. Unless her auntie's estate is large enough to pay an estate tax, no tax will be paid on the value of the asset. Margaret inherits the painting free of any tax, and the capital gains clock is reset, with the value of the painting starting at $110,000. Should Margaret someday sell the painting, she would pay a capital gains tax only on the increase in value in excess of its stepped-up basis of $110,000.

Under the carryover scheme, Margaret would inherit the painting with a $100,000 capital gains liability. Should the asset be sold, a capital gains tax would be paid on any profit over Aunt Margaret's original cost of $10,000. That old basis is carried over. Although President Kennedy proposed the change, Congress didn't take up the issue until 1976, as part of sweeping tax reform legislation. The 1976 bill included a provision eliminating the stepped-up basis and replacing it with the carryover basis. This provision, however, had a rather mysterious demise.

After passing both houses of Congress and receiving final approval by a conference committee, the Senate failed to enact it. The Revenue Act of 1978 delayed the implementation of the provision until 1980, at which time it was repealed. According to a Congressional Research Service report, the primary rationale for eliminating the carryover basis was a concern that it resulted in greater administrative burdens for estates, heirs, and the Treasury Department.[79] Determining the original cost on many items in estates would prove challenging.[80] The documentation on original cost of many items, including land, artwork, stamp collections, fishing boats, stocks, businesses, simply doesn't exist, or it goes back many generations. The existing step-up basis at death provision makes life a lot easier. It enables each generation to start over with a clean slate in terms of capital gains liability.

As we'll see later, the 2001 tax bill eventually repeals the estate tax and replaces it with carryover basis. The same difficult issues in administering the tax will exist, as well as continued opposition by the wealthy. We suspect that when the time comes this provision will also be politically unpopular, prove unmanageable, and will never be implemented.[81]

The Tax Reform Act of 1976 also made other significant changes to the estate tax to close loopholes, reduce rates, raise exemptions, and create new ones (such as a special exemption for real estate used in farms and other closely held businesses). The 1976 act created a unified estate and gift tax framework that consisted of a single, graduated rate. It also introduced what is called the Generation Skipping Tax, aimed at avoiding the impact of generation-skipping trusts at reducing estate taxes. Additional rules governing the Generation Skipping Tax were adopted in 1986, making it very expensive to attempt to reduce taxation by passing wealth to grandchildren rather than to children.[82]

Later in 1981, Congress passed the Economic Recovery Tax Act, reopening the floodgates to enormous tax reductions and loopholes. At this time, the estate tax was modified to allow spouses to inherit the entirety of their deceased spouses' estate without paying any estate taxes, a major change, but still preserving the step-up in basis for the entire estate tax-free inheritance received from the deceased spouse.

The modern effort to abolish the estate tax was born in the early 1990s. As we shall discuss in the next chapter, these efforts laid the groundwork for estate tax repeal in 2001. One incremental step toward repeal was the passage of three estate tax reforms as part of the 1997 Taxpayer Relief Act. First was the establishment of a schedule for increasing the effective exemption from $625,000 in 1998 to $1 million in 2006. A second provision legislated new exclusions for qualified family-owned businesses, responding to allegations that the estate tax contributed to the demise of family-owned enterprises. A third provision responded to concerns that the estate tax was forcing the sale of environmentally significant lands. The 1997 act permitted estates to exclude up to 40 percent of the value of land that met conservation, preservation, or education criteria, as well as allowing a charitable deduction for part of the land as well.

CHAPTER THREE

Opposition to the Estate Tax

On a sunny March morning, we were waiting to meet with Maine senator Olympia Snowe to discuss the estate tax issue. While flipping through newspapers, we encountered full-page advertisements in both the *Wall Street Journal* and the *Washington Times* that leapt out at us. "Don't Believe the Elitist Millionaire Con," declared the banner headline.

In the center of the advertisement was a picture of a young woman under the organizational banner of Disabled Americans for Death Tax Relief. The woman was Erin O'Leary, a thirty-year-old woman with multiple sclerosis who was "deeply offended by the callous and heartless comments made by 125 so-called 'millionaire'" signers of the Responsible Wealth ad that appeared in the *New York Times*."[1]

The text of the advertisement was a first-person letter from O'Leary. She pointed out that there are 2.5 million disabled people who are family members of millionaires, a number that would grow to 8 million over the next thirty years. With rising medical costs, these individuals needed their inheritances. The text of the advertisement continued:

> Some of us who would receive this wealth are in wheelchairs. Some are deaf and blind. Some are on respirators. Others require medication or nursing services. In order to live a full life, these Americans may require medical help, nursing and living assistance far beyond

that which is covered by medical insurance. Warren Buffet, Bill Gates, Sr. and George Soros believe that these people should be denied full financial help from their parents.

In the Call to Preserve the Estate Tax, we wrote that that repeal of the estate tax would leave an "unfortunate legacy for future generations," particularly in terms of the shifting tax burden. This advocate of repeal twisted the meaning of our statement and responded, "I take offense that this group of wealthy elite should term helping people like me an 'unfortunate legacy.'"

O'Leary claimed that she had just formed her organization and had "recruited over 1,000 supporters just in the last two weeks." Then the advertisement narrative took a bizarre twist.

> When I was younger, I dreamed of working for the FBI. But despite a degree in criminal psychology, I had to put aside my dream—because my multiple sclerosis contributes to occasional bouts of paralysis and problems with my balance and depth perception. I have tried to make the best of the situation. Today, I am a registered private investigator, and in fact, I used my resources to learn more about the people who signed the *New York Times* ad.
>
> The 125 signers are anything but a cross-section of America's wealthy. Nor are they even remotely bi-partisan. Democrats outnumber Republicans 20–1. The four Republican signers of the *New York Times* ad are even outnumbered by signers who contributed to Ralph Nader's presidential campaign.
>
> As to the wealth of these people and their ability to leave money to their children—a large percentage of them don't even have a child. Many of the others do not remotely qualify as millionaires.

We were stunned and fascinated. We ourselves had never surveyed the 1,100 signers of the call and wondered how, in one month's time, she had sleuthed to discover such detailed information as whether or not our signers had children.

We were also astonished by the exaggerated claims of the number of disabled people potentially affected. Less than fifty thousand estates a year pay the estate tax. So even if every estate had a disabled heir, it would take 160 years to reach the 8 million mark.

Fortunately, most news media recognized the organization for the charade that it was. Everyone except the Fox network, who kept O'Leary busy with interviews on programs such as the O'Reilly Factor and a Special Report with Brit Hume. When Fox News invited us to debate O'Leary, we declined and suggested they invite one of several national leaders from the disability rights movement. These leaders would ask the question: If we keep cutting taxes, how will we afford to pay for the medical services needed by the 98 percent of disabled people who don't have wealthy parents?

The proponents of repeal had struck again. Clearly there were few limits to their imagination, obfuscation, and resources. This was one of several amazing lines of attack that we encountered in our effort to broaden our nation's discussion about the estate tax.

During the heat of the 2001 tax debate, we never really understood the powerful forces we were up against. But we knew they were effective. By the time our coalition came together in February 2001 to oppose repeal, it was clear that the proponents of repeal had locked down support with a substantial majority in the House of Representatives and a slim majority in the Senate.

Occasionally we got a fleeting glimpse into the opposition's awesome media and mobilization capacity. But it was as if we were shadowboxing against a powerful opponent we didn't know. Reform organizers lacked the time and resources to research the repeal forces, learn their strategies, and assess their resource base.

Since June 2001, we've been able to research and talk to leaders of the repeal forces and have begun to patch together a picture of their operations. We've developed a grudging appreciation for their tenacity and willingness to toil, for over a decade, in their quest for absolute abolition.

What follows is a brief sketch of the opposition—a case study of narrow special interest politics.

THE EFFORT TO REPEAL THE ESTATE TAX

Ten years ago, it must have seemed a Don Quixote–like mission to galvanize interest and support for eliminating a federal tax provision that touched only a minuscule and wealthy fraction of the population.

As with any effort to change public policy, there are myriads of organizations, coalitions, researchers, and legislative leaders, each playing a part in abolishing the estate tax. Not surprisingly, the conservative think tanks and lobbying firms in our nation's capital played a central role in generating reports, working the media, and funneling campaign contributions to legislators. There were several other organizational and geographical power centers in what columnist E. J. Dionne calls the "pro-inherited wealth lobby," including Washington, D.C.; Orange County, California; and Seattle, Washington.

INSIDE THE D.C. BELTWAY

The Bush tax proposal of 2001 brought forth the special interest feeding frenzy that historically occurs around congressional tax writing. In *Showdown at Gucci Gulch,* a riveting account of the 1986 tax reform effort, Jeffrey Birnbaum and Alan Murray provide a window into the firepower of special interest politics.[2] "Gucci Gulch" refers to the hallway outside of the two key congressional tax-writing chambers, the House Ways and Means Committee and the Senate Finance Committee. There lobbyists wander in search of a senator willing to insert a strategic phrase or delayed activation date into a tax bill, thereby saving their corporate clients millions in taxes.

In the spring of 2001, President Bush had called off the business lobbyists, discouraging them from loading a tax bill written to benefit individuals with their wish list of special corporate subsidies, loopholes, and provisions. They were encouraged to wait until after the president's first tax bill had passed. They eventually mobilized in the fall of 2001, when the nation debated an economic stimulus package to respond to war and recession. But during the spring of 2001, the corporate tax lobby was free to devote its efforts to repeal.[3]

Unfortunately the people who pay estate taxes are also the

very people who can pay to have it repealed. As with other special interest legislation, those who are most affected are overwhelmingly involved in advocating for their narrow provisions—while the public is unaware and unorganized to defend the common interest. There is no lobby of ordinary citizens standing vigil to ensure the fairness of the tax code.

Yet in Washington, D.C., there is a whole industry of antitax lobbying organizations, think tanks, public opinion research, and communications experts—combined with spigots of money to advance the interests of a narrow slice of the population.

Although at times these organizations work at cross-purposes, when it comes to cutting taxes and shrinking government, they march in formation. The Heritage Foundation, the Cato Institute, and the American Enterprise Institute generate arguments in the form of studies, opinion pieces, and talking points. They share this information with their colleagues who host talk radio programs and write columns. Their public relations firms develop and place advertisements, running from the Disabled Americans for Death Tax Relief to local radio advertisements attacking legislators who advocate for estate tax reform but not for repeal.

Several national antitax lobby groups were part of the fight to repeal the estate tax. The central organizations included the Americans for Tax Reform, National Federation of Independent Business, Citizens for a Sound Economy, and Club for Growth, a lobbying spin-off from the libertarian Cato Institute. These organizations then formed coalitions such as Small Business Survival Committee, the Family Business Estate Tax Coalition, and several other ad hoc groups to oppose the estate tax—each with its own staff, lobbyists, and media consultants. They hired sophisticated lobbying firms such as Patton Boggs, Miller & Chevailier, and Ernst & Young to troll the Capitol hallways and funnel money to legislative leaders such as Representative Christopher Cox (R-Calif.) and Representative Jennifer Dunn (R-Wash.), who led the estate tax repeal cause in Congress.[4]

"DEATH TAX": WHAT'S IN A NAME?

The proponents of estate tax abolition have a good thing going for them with the moniker "death tax." Language is essential to enlisting popular support. After President Reagan's missile defense program was dubbed "star wars," proponents had difficulty regaining control over the terms of the debate.[5]

Defenders of the estate tax lost the battle of shibboleths early on. We knew we were in trouble in 2000, when major television news networks, such as CNN, abandoned objectivity, using "death tax" rather than estate tax in their news coverage.

The derivation of the "death tax" phrase is disputed, with several individual pollsters and lobbyists taking credit for coining the successful tag.[6] As it turns out, the phrase "death tax" has been around for several decades, but it came into popular use in the mid-1990s, thanks to concerted efforts to focus the repeal campaign message.

California congressman Christopher Cox (R-Calif.), a lead sponsor of repeal legislation, notes that there were many references to "death taxes" in professional tax journals dating back to the 1970s. Californians, who repealed their state inheritance tax in 1982, deployed the "death tax" phrase throughout the campaign.[7] President Reagan first used the term in a Minnesota speech in 1982.[8]

One significant player in advancing the "death tax" tag was Jim Martin, a longtime activist who founded "60 Plus," a conservative Washington beltway alternative to the American Association of Retired Persons. Although mostly concerned with privatizing Social Security, 60 Plus jumped headlong into the crusade against the estate tax.

Martin has the distinction of having given President George W. Bush his first political job. When Bush was twenty-two years old, Martin hired him to work on the 1968 campaign in Florida to elect Ed Gurney to Congress. The president, distinguished for his unique nicknames of friends and colleagues, calls Martin "Buddha."[9]

Martin is credited with having brought the "death tax" coin back into wider circulation in 1993. He gained an ally in political mastermind Frank Luntz. Luntz, who conducted focus groups for conservative causes and politicians, understood the importance of language. He even wrote a rhetoric primer for conservative politicians with the Orwellian name "Language for the Twenty-first Century."

Luntz's message research found that "death tax" kindled voter resentment in a way that "inheritance tax" and "estate tax" didn't. Luntz shared his findings with Republican leaders and included the phrase in the GOP's 1994 "Contract with America."

In a strategy memo to GOP lawmakers, the media-savvy Luntz suggested that legislators stage press conferences opposing the estate tax "at your local mortuary" to dramatize the issue. "I believe this backdrop will clearly resonate with your constituents," advised Luntz. "Death is something the American people understand."[10]

The first challenge of any campaign is to have a good message. But it is another hurdle, as the media spin masters will tell you, to enforce "message discipline" (i.e., getting everyone to say the same thing). Enter the pizza fund.

Across Washington, D.C., by water coolers in lobbying organizations, the hard-won battle for message discipline was waged. Woe to the innocent office intern or researcher who referred to the "death tax" as "the estate tax" or by its proper name, "the Federal Estate and Gift Tax and Generation-Skipping Transfer Tax." For this transgression, a one-dollar fine was levied to the pizza fund. The amount collected would pay for a periodic pizza party.

"Death tax pizza funds" first appeared at Jim Martin's 60 Plus organization. Then, across the Potomac, a pizza fund was instituted by Jack Faris, the president and CEO of the National Federation of Independent Business. Soon the idea spread to Capitol Hill, where then House Speaker Newt Gingrich and other pro-repeal lawmakers instituted pizza funds in their offices.

Slowly the powerful "death tax" phrase worked itself out from these lobbying groups into advertising, talk shows, and into the title of legislation, the "Death Tax Elimination Act of 2000." A powerful message catapulted the repeal cause forward.

ORANGE COUNTY, CALIFORNIA

Some of the earliest organizing for estate tax abolition started in Orange County, California, location of several of the most affluent zip codes in America. Early in the 1990s, a Santa Ana–based financial planner and political operative named Patricia Soldano enlisted support for an education and lobbying effort to terminate the estate tax.

Patricia Soldano and her firm, Cymric, set up "family offices" for affluent families to advise them on estate and other financial planning matters. Over the years, she developed a significant roster of well-resourced clients, including, according to her promotional materials, the Brown family of California, the Plimpton family of New Jersey, and the Field family of Illinois.[11]

In the early 1990s, Soldano took steps outside her business to, in her words, "advance the interests of Cymric client families." In 1992, she founded the Center for the Study of Taxation, a nonprofit, tax-exempt 501(c)(3) corporation, to research the "adverse effects on families and the economy caused by the estate, gift and generation skipping tax." The center produced publications such as a sixteen-page booklet advocating repeal and managed a Web site with numerous fact sheets and "horror stories" of people who had to pay the estate tax.

The center's Web site includes "talking points" for its activists, many with distorted allegations and misinformation. The center instructs its advocates to talk about the "value to Washington (of the estate tax) and the cost to families."

> Americans are surprised to learn that the estate tax raises a little more than one percent of total Federal revenues and costs are of the same magnitude. To personalize these stats, then add, "Though they account for only one percent of Federal revenues, estate taxes have

forced the sale of thousands of farms, ranches, and businesses throughout this country, and we can only guess at the jobs and economic potential lost."[12]

As we shall discuss later, many of these assertions are wildly inaccurate. The center's Web site urges opponents of the estate tax to adopt the "jobs argument": "Economists calculate that if the money paid in estate taxes in 1999 [were] invested instead, total savings in 2010 would be $1.7 trillion higher, the economy would be $137.2 billion larger, and we would have 275,000 more jobs." As we shall discuss later, these estimates are based on some rather grandiose assumptions.

In 1996, Soldano formed the Policy and Taxation Group, a lobbying organization "dedicated to the repeal of the estate, gift and generation skipping tax, providing an outlet for families interested in communicating their concerns to members of Congress." The group's donors consisted of wealthy families across the country, including heirs of the Mars candy fortune, the Gallo winery, and a number of investment corporations.[13] This "outlet" became a gushing river. Over the years, Soldano received between $250,000 and $500,000 a year to do direct lobbying and pay for the services of D. C. beltway lobbying firms such as Patton Boggs.[14] This did not include the hundreds of thousands of dollars in direct political contributions her clients made to congressional representatives to advance the cause.

According to the Center on Responsive Politics, Patton Boggs is the seventh-largest contributor of funds to congressional campaigns. In 1999, the most recent year for data, some of the groups that paid almost $18 million to retain Patton Boggs lobbying services included America Online ($120,000), 3M Company ($340,000) and Mars Inc. ($620,000).

Among Soldano's longtime lobbying patrons are the Gallo family, one of America's most well known wine producers. The Gallo family is no stranger to the world of tax and government policy, nor have they been hesitant to spend money to lobby for their parochial interests. In 1986, their lobbyists inserted provisions about the estate tax into the 1986 tax reform bill, including what became known as the "Gallo amendment"—an exception that would allow the Gallo children to inherit more than $80 million without paying a generation-skipping transfer tax.[15]

One of the earliest legislative leaders on the estate tax repeal effort was Representative Christopher Cox, also from Orange County. In July 1993, Cox introduced the Family Heritage Preservation Act to immediately repeal the estate tax. In the first two years, he enlisted twenty-nine cosponsors of his legislation in the House.

Throughout the 1990s, Representative Cox reintroduced his bill each year. And each year the Taxation and Policy Group, along with other lobbyists and operatives, enlisted more cosponsors. In 1994, estate tax repeal was included as part of the GOP's "Contract with America," and momentum increased as conservatives swept to power in the U.S. House and Senate. By 1998, Cox had 206 cosponsors, including the entire GOP leadership.[16]

SEATTLE, WASHINGTON

Lane Kirkland, the former president of the AFL-CIO, advised "never getting into an argument with people who buy printing ink by the barrel."[17] In opposing wholesale repeal of the estate tax, however, we not only crossed swords with a prominent newspaper publisher but also ran afoul of an entire association of newspaper owners.

One of the most passionate and committed organizers against the estate tax is Seattle's Frank Blethen. Blethen is the fourth-generation publisher of the *Seattle Times* and owner of several other daily newspapers in Washington State and in Maine. In the late 1990s, he bought three independent newspapers in Maine, including the state's largest newspaper, the *Portland Press Herald*. He cited an ancestral interest in Maine, the birthplace of his great-grandfather.[18]

Blethen believes the estate tax is a direct threat to his publishing business remaining family-owned, private, and independent. As a result, he has marshaled his considerable energy and resources to this cause. The fact that repeal efforts have advanced as far as they have is a credit to his talents and tenacity.

Blethen deployed the *Seattle Times* and his other newspapers to advance the repeal agenda. He hired Jill Mackie as director of external affairs at the *Times,* whose top mandate was to lobby for repeal. Blethen newspapers have editorialized against the tax numerous times since 1997 and in favor of candidates who share their pro-repeal position. The *Seattle Times* staffed an imaginative Web site (*www.deathtax.com*) that served as a hub of information and campaign activity.[19]

One of the most important things that the *Seattle Times* did was to organize other independent newspapers. It sent out frequent newsletters and lobbying updates to the thirty members of the Pacific Northwest Newspaper Association and organized at least one hundred other independent newspapers to join the repeal cause.[20] The paper reached out to enlist minority newspaper publishers, including M. Alexis Scott, the publisher of the African-American *Atlanta Daily World,* and Alejandro Aguirre, of the Miami-based *Diario Las Americas.* Without diverse publishers, Blethen explained, "it sure wasn't going to cut any ice with Democrats."[21]

Starting in 1997, the *Seattle Times* convened annual "Death Tax Summits" in Washington, D.C., with cosponsorship from the Newspaper Association of America, the U.S. Chamber of Commerce, and various other groups supporting repeal of the estate tax. At these events, business owners could hear from "congressional champions" and lobby representatives, and later they could join a reception with "those who work for repeal daily in Washington." We wonder if they served free pizza.[22]

Blethen enlisted George Duff, retired president of the Seattle Chamber of Commerce, to mount a lobbying campaign. Blethen and Duff did active targeting and lobbying. In one newsletter, they report that Washington State congressional candidate (now U.S. Representative) Brian Baird "fully understands this issue, having been initially schooled on it by Ted Natt," owner of the *Daily News* in Longview, Washington. In another lobbying roundup, they report that

[Democratic] Senator Patty Murray is also very versed on the issue and very supportive. However, she feels she is stuck with the current Congressional Budget Office (CBO) scoring of something like $100 billion of revenue loss for the Dunn/Tanner repeal bill. She understands that the CBO numbers are not valid, and in fact the death tax hurts the economy. However, she points out that Congress is stuck with them and she is willing to work to try to get CBO to reduce their scoring. Any calls to Murray would also be very helpful.[23]

Hundreds of these independent newspapers ran editorials advocating repeal, but they were hardly disinterested parties to the debate.

The activism of these independent newspapers was not limited to the opinion page. Several times a year, starting in 1997, the *Seattle Times* produced full-page advertisements against the estate tax. These advertisements were circulated in camera-ready and electronic formats to other newspaper publishers. As one *Seattle Times* "Death Tax newsletter" reported, "The ads are vertical, half page formal and can be downloaded and run with your newspaper's logo inserted or can be attributed to the Family Business Estate Tax Coalition, a group of nearly 100 national business associations advocating repeal."[24]

These advertisements, many of which can still be viewed at a "death tax" Web site run by the *Seattle Times,* were full of distortions and misinformation. For example, several advertisements alleged that "the IRS spends 65 cents for every dollar it collects from the tax." This misinformation was repeated as recently as May 2001 in a *Seattle Times* editorial (and again during the 2002 debate). In 1999, the IRS collected $28 billion in estate taxes, and the *entire* IRS budget covering all tax revenue (not just the estate tax) that year was $8 billion.[25]

The Web site and advertising, which are created and maintained by the *Seattle Times,* fall far short of objective journalism. One advertisement alleges that "independent studies reveal that [repeal] would actually help reduce the deficit." Although there is one study that imagines a trickle-down surge in net tax revenue as the result of repeal, most studies find that abolishing the tax would be expensive. The site, which was primarily concerned with the plight of "family businesses," stated that only $650,000 of an inheritance can be exempted from taxation, omitting the exemption for married couples, which at the time was $1.3 million, and the generous valuation standards available to qualified family-owned businesses.[26]

These misrepresentations were not simple misquotations or one-time mistakes. These advertisements and Web site allegations became source material for many repeal spokespeople. This misinformation appeared over and over on fact sheets and was repeated by legislative leaders like Representative Jennifer Dunn of Washington State and Senator Jon Kyl of Arizona.

Misinformation or not, as many as one hundred newspapers ran these advertisements in each quarter, compliments of their owners. This is a staggering amount of publicity for an issue, in the form of both free advertising and opinion page inches.

Clearly the enormous power of these newspapers to shape opinion was not lost upon the elected officials from the jurisdictions served by these publications. This power was likely considered in Maine, for instance, where its two senators were critical key swing votes on the tax bill. It would not be prudent to ignore the editorial wishes of three major newspapers in your state.

These are not ordinary citizens with a grievance. They own printing presses, underscoring A. J. Leibling's oft-quoted aphorism that "freedom of the press is guaranteed only to those who own one."

HIDING THE REAL FACE OF ESTATE TAXPAYERS

The estate tax is central in the debate over taxes, not only because the sums involved are huge but also because it is a touchstone of national values. To those seeking to abolish it, the estate tax is a penalty for success, an abomination that blocks the deeply human desire to leave a life's work as a legacy for the children. It is also a complicated burden that enriches the lawyers, accountants and life insurance companies that help people reduce their tax bills.

To its supporters, on the other hand, the estate tax is a symbol

of American equality, a mechanism to democratize society and to
encourage economic success based on merit rather than birthright.
Yet for all the passion in the debate the estate tax does not always
seem broadly understood.

—David Cay Johnston[27]

We'd like to examine the case for repeal as articulated by its most
active proponents. In the heat of a policy debate, many of their assertions and allegations went unanswered and untested. A deeper
probe of the evidence, however, reveals a lot of obfuscation and
mythology. And where the information is inconclusive, we hope
to stimulate additional research and discussion.

The estate tax should not be repealed based on the paltry public debate that our country had in 2001 and 2002. Our nation's investigative reporters, researchers, and pundits should do better to
sort through the conflicting claims and allegations about the estate tax.

At the heart of the repeal campaign was a systematic distortion
of the facts as to who pays the estate tax and who would benefit
from wholesale repeal. Here we refer to the assertion that small
farmers and family businesses are those most affected by the estate tax.

The architects of the repeal effort are true believers. They believe that nothing short of complete repeal is satisfactory and oppose any reform or compromise. In their all-or-nothing crusade
for repeal, the proponents mobilized their farm and small business
constituencies, without informing them about reform options.

Reforms, such as dramatically raising the amount of wealth
exempted, will address the concerns of the tiny sliver of affected
farmers and bona fide small business owners touched by the estate
tax. Repeal advocates understand that such reforms will rob proponents of any popular case for repeal and will not help the principal patrons of the repeal effort, the very wealthy interests who
bankrolled the campaign.

Imagine a series of advertisements with profiles of the true
beneficiaries of estate tax repeal. Picture a group of third-genera-
tion millionaires, teenagers draped in Armani clothes and jewelry,

standing in front of their mansions and fancy cars. One of them earnestly pleads, "I've never worked a day in my life and I'm hoping I never to have to. Please repeal the estate tax."

Another teenager says, "We're worried our $1 million dollar inheritance plus our debt-free college education won't be enough of a head start in today's world."

Another advertisement could reveal the true family business interests behind the repeal effort. "My family started the Acme Corporation and I would like to inherit $140 million in appreciated stock without paying taxes. Please help me by repealing the estate tax."

Obviously, the plight of these beneficiaries would not inspire great public sympathy. The proponents of repeal understand that to win the hearts and minds of the American public they cannot reveal these real beneficiaries of repeal. Instead, they manufactured more compelling stories and chose small farmers and owners of family-owned businesses to be the visible faces of their advertising campaign for repeal. During the spring of 2001, opponents staged press events with women, widows, disabled Americans, and owners of minority-owned businesses—but omitted those most likely to pay the tax: wealthy white multimillionaires and their children.

THE ESTATE TAX DOWN ON THE FARM

Many family farms must be sold off to pay the Federal taxes due on the property. Its just plain wrong.
—Center for Tax Policy Web site

The product of a life's work leaches away like seeds in poor soil.
—Senator Charles E. Grassley (R-Iowa) referring to the estate tax[28]

To keep farms in the family, we are going to get rid of the death tax!
—Candidate George W. Bush on the campaign trail in Iowa, 2000[29]

During the spring of 2001, a number of investigative reporters began to question the allegation that small farmers were the principal victims of the estate tax. Prior to that time, small farmers were the public relations icons in the campaign to abolish the tax. Anti–estate tax literature was so full of images of working farmers that they looked like centerfolds from *Successful Farming* magazine.

Throughout pro-repeal literature are allegations that the estate tax has forced working farmers to sell their farms. There are stories of ranch families whose parents, without an estate tax plan in place, met an untimely death. They testify how they were forced to borrow money or sell cattle to pay the tax.

In the summer of 2000, Congress passed a complete repeal bill for the first time. To underscore the "down on the farm" image, proponents arranged for a rancher named Lynn Cornwell of Glasgow, Montana, to deliver the estate tax repeal bill from Congress to the White House on a "borrowed tractor." Cornwell, president of the National Cattlemen's Beef Association, told reporters that "the threat of having a tax like this takes away all incentive of growing your business."[30] Clearly, a bright red tractor wandering through the district's busy streets provided good television and photo copy to dramatize the connection between farmers and the estate tax.

On August 31, 2000, President Clinton vetoed the Death Tax Elimination Act of 2000, responding that it would primarily enrich the heirs of estates in excess of $5 million. "Half the benefit of that bill that came here on a tractor goes to 3,000 people," quipped President Clinton. "And I'll bet you not a single one of them ever drove a tractor." Clinton went on to boast, "I'll bet you if I had a tractor-driving contest with any of those 3,000 people, I would win."[31] Senate minority leader Richard A. Gephardt observed that "if Republicans were being honest about the beneficiaries of their estate tax break, it would have been delivered by Donald Trump in a stretch limo, not a farmer on a tractor."[32]

True stories of farmers losing the farm to the estate tax are so rare that numerous experts and investigators were unable to find any real examples. Neil Harl, an Iowa State University economist whose tax advice has made him a household name among Midwest farmers, said he had searched far and wide but had never found a case in which a farm was lost because of estate taxes. "It's a myth," said Harl, "M-Y-T-H."[33]

Lloyd A. Brown, president of Hertz Farm Management in the town of Nevada, Iowa, runs more than four hundred farms in ten states. He maintains that none of his clients nor anyone he knew was facing farm loss problems because of the estate tax.[34]

New York Times reporter David Cay Johnston, who won a Pulitzer Prize in 2001 for his investigative reporting on federal tax policy, spent a week in Iowa in search of farmers who had lost farms because of the estate tax. He asked officials from the pro-repeal American Farm Bureau Federation to provide examples of farms that were lost because of estate taxes. They could not cite one example.

Johnston interviewed dozens of farmers who explained that the estate tax was irrelevant to them either because of the low valuation of their farms or because of the ease in planning for the estate tax. One Iowa farm family, Harlyn and Karen Riekena, estimate the value of their farm to be $2.5 million and have undertaken a simple plan. They make annual gifts to their daughters and purchase life insurance to offset any estate taxes that might be due if they die before most of their 950 acres of corn and soybeans is transferred to their daughters.

Riekena and the two dozen other farmers interviewed across central Iowa, every one a Republican, said that while they favored increasing the amount that could be passed to heirs untaxed, they did not support the repeal proposed by President Bush and other leaders of his party. "A few snickered or laughed" when Johnston asked whether the estate tax should be repealed to save the family farm. "For most farmers around here, the estate tax is not high in their minds," Riekena said. "What we need are better crop prices."[35]

Several investigative reporters in other states repeated the same query and found similar results. Other reporters asked repeal proponents and the American Farm Bureau Federation to produce a single example of a farm lost because of the estate tax. Once again, they couldn't produce a single example. On April 19, the American Farm Bureau Federation put out an urgent call to state farm bureaus trying to recruit examples. In a memo to affiliates, federation president Bob Stallman wrote, "It is crucial for us to be able to provide Congress with examples of farmers and ranchers who have lost farms . . . due to the death tax." Still, no examples were forthcoming.[36]

Here's what we know about the facts. Only six in ten thousand estates each year involve significant farm assets. Data show that in 1997 and 1998 farm assets were reported on less than 6 percent of all taxable estates, and farm assets totaled 0.3 percent of taxable estate value. Farm real estate was reported on 12 percent of taxable returns, which seems like a high percentage. But together, farm assets and real estate constituted just 1.7 percent of all taxable estate value.[37]

Tax return data for 1999 show that there were 6,216 taxable estates (12.5 percent of all taxable estates) that showed any agricultural land and equipment. The average value of farm real estate and assets was $440,000, about one-third of what a married couple could leave untaxed to heirs in that year. Since then the exemptions have risen. As a result, almost no working farm estates owed estate tax according to data from the Internal Revenue Service analysis of 1999 returns.[38]

Under the 1997 Tax Reform Act, the estate tax was modified so that it was more favorable to farmers and small businesses. Under its more generous valuation terms, a farm couple can pass along as much as $4.1 million untaxed, as long as the heirs continue farming for ten years. Low-interest payment plans on fourteen-year terms further reduce the burden.[39]

In Iowa, the average farm has a net worth of $1.2 million. Only 1,222 estates (2.5 percent) exceeded that value, making them potentially subject to estate taxes under the pre-2001 increase in exemptions. As David Cay Johnston writes, "these farm assets amounted to one-tenth of these estates, suggesting that the tax applies mostly to gentleman farmers and ranchers, rather than to working farmers . . . whose fortunes are tied up in their farms."[40]

The cynicism of pro-repeal forces gets more unseemly when it appears that the same pro-repeal lobbies and politicians have consistently opposed other legislation that would have helped active small farmers. Apparently some of the most strident proponents of repeal are moved to aid small farmers only after they die and have to pay estate taxes. Because while they are alive, the same congressional leaders are supporting farm policies that are devastating to family farms.

Senator Jon Kyl (R-Ariz.), who intones the plight of small farmers facing the "death tax," also supported farm legislation that has destroyed tens of thousands of family farms. Of the fifty-one senators who voted for complete repeal in July 2000, forty-nine of them also voted for the 1996 "Freedom to Farm" bill, farm policy legislation that some rural commentators described as the "death warrant" for family farming in America.[41]

The Federal Agricultural Improvement and Reform Act, dubbed "Freedom to Farm" by proponents, was touted as a way to increase exports and the price of crops. But according to the Minnesota-based Institute for Agriculture and Trade Policy, "Freedom to Farm" has failed miserably on both accounts.[42] "Freedom to Farm" further tilted U.S. agricultural policy in favor of the large agribusiness companies and factory-style farmers at the expense of family producers. This has accelerated a long and steep drop in the number of family farmers. The total number of farms in the United States has steadily declined from 6.5 million in 1935 to just over 2 million in 1997, with most of that decline among family farms.[43] Since the enactment of what some farmers now call "Freedom to Fail," the number of family farms "has gone into a free fall."[44]

The distribution of farm subsidies tells part of the story. During the farm bill debate of 2002, an informative Web site sponsored by the Environmental Working Group (www.ewg.org) revealed the allocation of farm subsidies since the 1996 "Freedom to Farm" bill. Over 70 percent of all farm subsidies now go to 10 percent of the farms, typically large-scale farms and ranches.[45] These big farms effectively use their subsidies to overproduce crops, create surpluses, and drive prices down, squeezing smaller farmers out of business. A *Wall Street Journal* editorial noted that "huge paychecks to agribusiness also drive up the cost of farmland, further driving out the little guys."[46] The big winners of these policies are the large grain buyers, who reap the harvest of depressed grain prices.

Without debating the intricacies of different farm policies, it is important to underscore that the real threats to stable family farming are not the estate tax. The estate tax has been used as a deflection or scapegoat for other agricultural policies. Lost in the debate about small farmers and the estate tax are the ways in which wholesale repeal would actually hurt working small farmers.

The primary threat to the survival of genuine family farming is the growing domination of megascale agriculture. Eliminating all estate taxes would only further concentrate agricultural assets into fewer hands. The real pressures facing small farmers are the prices they get for their products and the succession challenges of passing a farm on to the next generation that are unrelated to taxation. Farm policies tilted to the benefit of large corporate agribusiness and factory farms are the major threat cited by most small farmers.

The Center for Rural Affairs in Nebraska pointed out that half of all hog producers had been forced out of business since 1995. "It was not estate taxes that drove them from business, but rather the rapid expansion of mega-operations and their depressing effect on hog markets." Chuck Hassebrook, from the Center for Rural Affairs, makes an eloquent case for reforming the tax. "An effective estate tax helps modest family farms survive the growing pressures from big agribusiness," according to Hassebrook. "Estate taxes help level the playing field between typical family farmers, who must compete for land based on what they can earn from it, and wealthy heirs of large farms who compete mainly on the basis of their inheritance."[47]

Throughout U.S. history, farmers have been leading proponents of the estate tax. As discussed earlier, farmers during the Gilded Age understood the dangers of concentrated farmland and wealth and sought a remedy in the institution of an estate tax.[48]

For those few farmers concerned with the estate tax, further increases in the exemptions will eliminate the need and cost of planning. Yet the powerful interests behind repeal never let reform proposals get into the debate or on the table. The American Farm Bureau, largely controlled by large farm and ranching interests, never informed its members about the opportunities for reforming the law, short of repeal. And when it came time to compromise, it opposed and blocked reforms that would have protected small farmers.[49]

In the summer of 2000, President Clinton indicated that he would have signed estate tax reform legislation to immediately triple the exemptions and virtually exempt small and medium-sized family farms from the tax. He viewed such reform proposals as "targeted, fiscally responsible legislation to make the estate tax fairer, simpler and more efficient." But Congress gave the president only a complete repeal bill, which he regarded as "regressive, poorly targeted and expensive." Virtually all the proponents of complete repeal voted to oppose reforms that would have immediately helped smaller estates.[50]

In the spring of 2001, some congressional leaders put forward legislation to immediately raise exemptions to $3.5 million instead of waiting ten years to reach that threshold.[51] Versions of the same reform legislation were sponsored in June 2002. These reforms would have immediately provided relief to any of the alleged farm and business concerns that they claimed were tangled in the estate tax web. But these amendments were defeated. "All or nothing" proponents are willing to hold the smaller estate taxpayers hostage in their bid for wholesale repeal.

Would dramatically raising the exemptions to $3.5 million exclude all farms in the United States? The answer is yes, since most are already excluded. After exemptions rise under the new law, only the largest ranches and farms would still be required to do estate planning and face estate tax liabilities. But should all farmers be completely excluded? What about enormous mega-farms or ranches with ten thousand acres? The estate tax is still justified on these super farms and ranches, especially with all the protections that exist for truly small-scale enterprise.

Part of the justification lies in the enormous public investment that we as taxpayers make in agriculture. Historically, we have placed a high value on independent family farms and provided substantial cash subsidies as well as below-market rates for grazing rights.

One case in point is Montana rancher Lynn Cornwell, the man who delivered the 2000 repeal bill to President Clinton on a tractor to symbolize the alleged plight of farmers facing the estate tax. Between 1996 and 2001, Cornwell received $415,015 in direct cash farm subsidies. In 1999 alone, the Cornwell Ranch received $127,931. The Cornwell Ranch was in the top 10 percent of subsidy recipients in Montana, the elite group that received 55 percent of Montana's $1.82 billion in farm subsidies between 1996 and 2000.[52] This does not include the enormous indirect subsidy that taxpayers provide Cornwell by allowing him to graze his cattle on federally owned lands at below-market rates.[53] Federal grazing subsidies cost taxpayers upward of $460 million a year.[54] Remember, this is the man who complained that the estate tax "takes away all incentive of growing your business." Surely after millions of dollars in subsidies and "incentives," shouldn't the American taxpayer, a virtual equity partner in Cornwell Ranch, be able to recoup a small percentage of this value when the ranch transfers to the next generation and is worth more than several million dollars?

Most of the value in farm estates lies in appreciated land value, capital gains that have never been taxed. If farmland is protected through a conservancy or sale of development rights, then its assessment will rightfully be lower. But what about appreciated farmland in prime development areas? It seems appropriate to levy an estate tax on transfers of the largest agricultural properties as a way to tap untaxed capital gains and recapture agricultural subsidies.

The Montana situation is an interesting case study. Agricultural subsidies for the entire state of Montana, as in many regions, exceed annual farm income.[55] And yet in 1997, the most recent year with good data, only 154 Montana estates owed estate taxes, out of an average of 7,752 deaths annually during the 1990s. These estates paid a combined estate tax of $23.1 million, or an average of $150,000 each.[56] With the wealth exemption raised to $3.5 million, only roughly twenty-five Montana estates will owe the tax annually.[57]

A journalist friend was talking to a Midwest farm group about the adverse effects of the estate tax on farms. One farmer looked at the journalist and remarked, "You city slickers have really fallen for that one. Nobody I know has ever sold a farm to pay estate taxes, and nobody has been able to find a farmer like that."

The proposition that small family farmers are being squeezed out of existence by the estate tax does not stand up to scrutiny. During the spring of 2001, reform advocates began to chip away at the small farm justification for complete repeal. The media finally started to ask for proof. The truth about this farmer myth began to find daylight. As a result, the farmers began to disappear from pro-repeal arguments, press conferences, and literature, and proponents began to trumpet more loudly the impact of the estate tax on family business.

THE ESTATE TAX AND FAMILY-OWNED ENTERPRISES

Family owned newspapers are an endangered species. In 1910 there were 2,100 independently owned newspapers in the United States. This number dropped to 700 in 1980 and today stands at only 300 out of 1500 daily newspapers. The primary source of this decline is the estate tax which creates a crisis of liquidity and prevents the continuation of most family businesses.

—*Seattle Times* Death Tax Newsletter, April 15, 1998

Repeal of the tax would result in 145,000 new jobs over the first 9 years of repeal. And that doesn't include the countless jobs that would be saved if the death tax didn't force 70% of family and small businesses to liquidate or sell out after only one generation.

—*Seattle Times* Death Tax Newsletter, June 15, 1998

The Washington-based lobbyists for large corporate interests learned long ago that there is an understandable sympathy for small-scale enterprise in our country. "Small business" evokes the "mom and pop" corner store, the neighborhood restaurant, and the struggling entrepreneur with fewer than twenty employees. We know the challenges and stresses that these business undertakings encounter. Yet proponents of repeal are part of a larger business lobby that deliberately blurs the distinction between "small business" and "family" or "independent" business.

You might be surprised about the wide range of companies that consider themselves "family businesses." The proponents of repeal would like you to think about Joe's Luncheonette or Jane's Hair Salon. But the real "family businesses" behind estate tax repeal include several we have already mentioned, such as Gallo wines ($875 million), Blethen newspapers (over $400 million[58]), Mars Candy ($27 billion, owned by three family members), and Maine catalog outfitters L. L. Bean. They also include the Dorrances of Campbell's Soup ($6.5 billion shared by six grandchildren of founder John T. Dorrance) and the Johnsons of Johnson Wax (one heir alone worth $2.4 billion).[59]

Many "family businesses" are owned by extended families, employ thousands of people, and are worth hundreds of millions of dollars. These big family businesses have established a number of lobbying organizations that ostensibly speak for the minnows but carry a lot of water for the marlins, tunas, and whales. For publicity purposes, they recruit and provide media training for small business leaders that fit the common image of "small."

Proponents of repeal allege that the estate tax destroys family businesses or at least forces them to sell. One study suggested that the estate tax "is the leading cause of dissolution for thousands of family-run businesses" and that it consequently "inhibits economic efficiency and stifles innovation."[60]

The National Federation of Independent Business (NFIB), a vocal opponent of the estate tax, extrapolated from IRS data that "around 5,600 family businesses were sold or discontinued for estate tax reasons during the 1990s." They concede that most family-run firms properly plan for their succession, but succession and estate planning is a costly burden of high lawyer's fees and life insurance at an "average premium of $45,000 a year."[61]

Jim Hirni, lobbyist for NFIB, told reporters that the repeal bill was "the single best thing to happen to small business. . . . Estate taxes force the sale of 87% of all family businesses before they make it to the third generation."[62]

These claims that the estate tax is a major cause in business dissolution are wildly exaggerated. Apparently the estate tax is a scapegoat for a plethora of reasons why businesses fail, the vast majority being completely unrelated to tax policy. Even regarding businesses for which family succession is a possibility, estate taxes are a minor issue.

James Repetti, an estate planning consultant and law professor at Boston College, finds scant evidence that the estate tax is a business killer. Among an association of business tax experts, Repetti could not find one example where someone was forced to sell a business because of the estate tax. "People use insurance for that, they plan. A lot of [family-owned] businesses do fail in subsequent generations, but it's not because of the estate tax. It's because of the complexities of transferring management responsibilities to a younger generation."[63]

A close analysis finds that most studies about the impact of the estate tax on businesses are fueled by anecdotal evidence. Much of the survey evidence that is cited is based on people's stated future intentions rather than their actions. For instance, NFIB queried its members with questions like "Without the estate tax, would you expand your business? How many people would you hire?" Based on such stated intentions, they crafted their estimates of job losses under the estate tax.[64]

More comprehensive studies have found that 77 percent of business owners could pay estate tax without borrowing or having it affect their business. Most pay liabilities out of insurance, liquid assets, stocks, and bonds, without having to use any nonliquid assets or the business itself to pay estate taxes.[65] On average, business owners cover more than 80 percent of their projected estate tax liability without affecting the business. Brookings Institution researchers found that even these estimates surely understate the true percentage of businesses that can pass to recipients without fear of being broken up by the estate tax. This is because most studies don't factor in the reduced valuation of businesses or any other estate tax planning, which greatly increase the ability to pay the tax without adverse consequences for the business. They conclude that the vast majority of closely held businesses do not appear to face imminent demise because of estate tax considerations.[66]

The key question, when looking into the future, is this: As exemptions rise, how many family enterprises will have a net worth of $3.5 million and be unable to pay the estate tax when transferring assets to a family member? The Brookings Institution researchers find "little logic and evidence that suggests that the impact of estate taxes on family farms and businesses is a major concern."[67]

A number of reformers do *not* advocate for additional special exemptions for small farmers and family businesses, because they already receive special treatment under the estate tax. For instance, they can calculate taxable value of property at the current use value rather than at market value. This can greatly diminish the value of their business assets for tax purposes and dramatically reduce or eliminate their tax bill.

The 1997 reforms to the estate tax permit a special deduction for qualified family-owned farms and businesses when they constitute at least 50 percent of an estate. In addition to these favorable provisions, any estate tax liability due can be paid over fourteen years with only interest charged for the first four years, at the rate of 2 percent for the first $1 million of taxable assets, with below-market rates on higher amounts. The 2001 tax law further liberalizes this provision.

Small businesses already receive numerous income tax subsidies for making investments. And an enormous amount of net
worth, some 66 to 80 percent of value of family-owned businesses,
is made up of unrealized capital gains.[68] The estate tax is a legitimate mechanism to tax those gains that escape income taxation.

THE CASE FOR REPEAL: UNSOUND
AND MISLEADING ARGUMENTS

Its part of the great American system that we raise young people to
believe in family, in individual effort and in fairness. The death tax
assaults families, it creates a disincentive for hard work and savings
and it is fundamentally unfair and all Americans should be concerned about an unfair tax that penalizes families that build a
business or farm with their energies, efforts and savings.
——Tucker Eskew, press secretary for candidate
George W. Bush in September 2000[69]

Approximately 10 million people a year are affected by the tax.
They don't all pay it but these are the people who pay to have others
plan their estates, to buy insurance, to pay the accountants and the
lawyers, and the people who lose their jobs, as a result of the businesses that go out of business or the money that's paid for estate
planning, rather than employing people.
——Senator Jon Kyl (Arizona), CNN *Crossfire*[70]

From listening to the proponents of estate tax repeal, one is
tempted to conclude that the tax is the single greatest threat to
Western civilization. The implication is that this lowly transfer tax
has been the ruin of many honest and enterprising people.

As we have ascertained from our examination of the plight of
small farmers and family businesses, there is a lot of smoke blow-
ing through these allegations. Imagine the small fortunes that
public relations firms must have charged to create, test, and dis-
seminate this crafty case for estate tax repeal.

At the heart of the case against the estate tax is a fundamental
belief that the tax is unfair. We don't expect true believers to be

dissuaded from this creed, any more than the authors will be convinced to abandon their core values. But we hope that fair-minded people will see that arguments for eliminating the estate tax have not been adequately scrutinized.

Some of the opposition's arguments stem from different values or divergences in worldview and economic theory. Others are technical concerns that lack clear-cut research. And some of them are purposeful distortions. Our goal is to stimulate a more honest assessment of the advantages and disadvantages of the estate tax— while not withholding our own opinions.

IS THE ESTATE TAX UNFAIR BECAUSE DEATH SHOULD NOT BE A TAXABLE EVENT?

> A core principle behind repealing the Death Tax is the idea that people should not be further burdened at the most difficult time of their lives.
>
> —Center for Policy and Taxation[71]

> You should not have to visit the undertaker and the taxman on the same day.
>
> —Former House Speaker Newt Gingrich

The proponents of repeal feel there is something ghoulish about a tax that is assessed at death. But is a tax on accumulated wealth at death any worse than a tax on the wages of the living?

Going back to our cardinal assumption, we know there will be a federal government that will require revenue—to protect national security, run schools, offer health care, operate national parks, oversee airports, and so on. So looking across the available sources of revenue, a transfer tax on the super wealthy at death is among the most, well . . . painless.

What other tax would be fairer in this pantheon of taxes? Estate taxes compared with what? Wage taxation? Increased sales taxes? Consumption taxation? A return to nineteenth-century tariffs? A wealth tax imposed on the living? The alternative to taxing dead wealthy people is to tax living working people. Which is more fair?

There is no tax on death itself. The estate tax is a transfer tax imposed at death on individuals with significant accumulated assets and paid for by their heirs. Over 98 percent of the population is untouched by estate taxes at death. Their children will actually get a "death bonus" of having assets with unrealized capital gains "stepped up" in value and passed on without any taxation.[72]

Tax returns on an estate are not due until nine months after a death. Nor is the payment immediately due either. Death may trigger a tax liability, but payments can be made at a later time, and in the case of qualified family-owned farms and businesses, over a period of fourteen years. Estate tax liabilities can be effectively *prepaid*, via life insurance purchases tied to the expected tax liability.[73]

It is interesting to note that there is no such outrage or opposition to paying income taxes due on 401(k) and IRA balances at death. This is because these are considered deferred taxes. Yet the estate tax, in general, is also a deferred tax on unrealized capital gains.

Death "may be unpleasant to contemplate," note tax researchers William Gale and Joel Slemrod, but life's final chapter may actually be the best time to impose taxes—for a variety of "good administrative, equity, and efficiency reasons."[74]

Death may provide an appropriate time to impose taxes in several ways. First, the probate process at death is a time when an executor accounts for the accumulation of assets over a person's lifetime. There are few other occasions when such an accounting takes place. A wealth tax assessed while alive would require appraisals and assessments similar to those that take place at death.[75]

The complaints about taxation at death are, for the most part, rooted in an opposition to any form of progressive taxation. Taken out of context, a tax on accumulated wealth at death might seem undesirable. But compared with what? If we instituted a wealth tax, to be assessed while people are alive, you would surely hear passionate arguments about waiting until death!

IS THE ESTATE TAX UNFAIR BECAUSE IT PUNISHES SUCCESSFUL PEOPLE?

Estate tax supporters are sometimes accused of wanting to punish successful people. This is a tired canard that is invoked around any form of progressive taxation, not just the estate tax. The accusation suggests that if you advocate higher taxes on wealthier individuals, you are antagonistic to people becoming prosperous and want to punish those who have worked hard. This is patently not true.

Over twelve hundred future estate taxpayers signed the Responsible Wealth petition to preserve the estate tax, attesting that there are plenty of people who believe that those with the greatest ability to pay should pay a higher percentage of taxes. As we will discuss later, society plays an enormous role in creating the fertile soil for wealth creation, and society has a substantial claim, particularly on the most wealthy among us. This is not anti-success; it is pro-responsibility.

From those to whom much is given, much is expected. For us, the progressivity of the tax system is a core principle. The notion that the greatest tax burden should fall upon those with the most resources is a matter of fundamental fairness.

State and local taxes are already extremely regressive. State sales taxes, property taxes, and sin taxes—all fall disproportionately more on those least able to pay. On average, U.S. families in the poorest one-fifth of the population paid 12.5 percent of their incomes on state and local sales, excise, property, and income taxes. The wealthiest 1 percent of households paid an average rate of 7.9 percent of their incomes.[76]

The progressive nature of the federal tax system, though it has diminished over the last twenty years, is necessary to offset the regressivity of state and local taxes. The estate tax is one of the components that make the overall tax burden fairer.

WHY PENALIZE PEOPLE WHO LEAVE THEIR HARD-EARNED SAVINGS AND WEALTH TO THEIR CHILDREN?

Some have argued that the estate tax is unfair because people "work hard all their lives" and want to leave something for their children. This invocation of denying children a family legacy is a powerful strategy because it touches on people's protective instincts. But recognize that today a parent that has accumulated wealth of less than $1 million can transfer all of it to heirs without any tax. Then the spouse can do the same. A couple with five children can give each of their heirs a tax-free transfer of four hundred thousand dollars, a pretty good bonus in today's economy. Under the changes in the estate tax law, that amount for each of the four siblings will rise to $1.4 million in a few years.

But imagine a scenario in which the head of household dies without a surviving spouse and has an estate of $10 million. If there had been absolutely no gifts to children while he or she was alive, an unlikely scenario, there would still be a substantial $7 million to $8 million distribution to the heirs under current law.

Much has been written about the foibles of heirs receiving substantial inheritances. In chapter 5, we will briefly discuss the imprudence of such large inheritances for heirs. Some would argue that this is a personal and private matter. But when substantial wealth is changing hands, it is no longer a private family matter but something that has tremendous consequences for the entire society. Legal philosophers Liam Murphy and Thomas Nagel observe:

> The sense that the government "has no business" in our personal, nonmarket transactions is based on a mistake. Good government makes a flourishing personal life possible just as much as it does civil society. But there comes a point where private transactions in their cumulative effects make a difference that is publicly important, and society must take notice. At that point, the personal becomes political and leaves the private sphere that is rightly protected against government intrusion. Most interpersonal gifts do not generate large economic consequences, but the intergenerational transmission of real wealth does; it cannot claim the protection of privacy against taxation to the recipient.[77]

This goes to the core notion of a democratic society's claim on the accumulated assets of the wealthy. As we will discuss later, people who have large net worth in this country owe a great deal to society and the social framework that we've built together, through our public investment and private institutions, to enable wealth creation by individuals.

IS THE ESTATE TAX A FORM OF DOUBLE TAXATION?

> Its irritating that once I die, 55% of my money goes to the U.S. government. You know why that's irritating? Because you would have already paid nearly 50%.

—Oprah Winfrey

> The estate tax is imposed on earnings and assets that have already been subject to income, social security, and other taxes at the federal and state level.

—Patricia Soldano[78]

Double taxation is the complaint of those who feel as though they've had to go through two tollbooths to pay for the same stretch of road. It is a common complaint in antitax circles.

When it comes to the estate tax, some people are concerned that they have already paid income or other taxes on the money that they have saved. Perhaps they have paid some capital gains taxes over their lifetime. So when it finally comes time to die, and pass on assets, there is another toll. No one wants to feel they are double-taxed or triple-taxed.

But the bulk of assets that are taxed in people's estates take the form of appreciated property that has not been taxed at all. The largest percentage of taxable estates are stocks and real estate in which there are substantial capital gains that have never been taxed.

In April 2001, a notable group of African-American business leaders took out full-page advertisements to call for repeal of the estate tax. Their lead spokesman was Robert Johnson, founder of Black Entertainment Television (BET). The first point of their advertisement states, "The Estate Tax is unfair double taxation since taxpayers are taxed twice—once when the money is earned and again when you die."[79]

Robert Johnson, however, is an excellent example of someone

for whom a substantial portion of his wealth has never been taxed. "They talk about the injustice of double and triple taxation," noted economist Julianne Malveaux, "without noticing that some of their assets have never been taxed. When Bob Johnson, for example, does a stock swap with Viacom, not a dollar, nor a tax liability, changes hands."[80] A stock swap is a way that many companies merge or buy one another out. Instead of paying Robert Johnson cash for the purchase of Black Entertainment Television, Johnson gave Viacom a controlling interest worth appreciated BET stock—and Viacom gave him appreciated Viacom stock. Johnson became a billionaire without paying taxes on his paper fortune. Upon his death, it is appropriate that his estate pay some taxes.

Estimates by economists James Poterba and Scott Weisbenner, based on data from the Survey of Consumer Finances, suggest that unrealized capital gains make up about 37 percent of the value of estates worth between $1 million and $10 million and over 56 percent of estates worth more than $10 million. In the case of family-owned businesses, several studies suggest that between 66 and 80 percent of the value of such enterprises are unrealized capital gains.[81]

For 98 percent of the population, any capital gains growth is exempted at death, as assets pass to decedents and the basis of their value is "stepped up" to their current value. Two tax experts, Joseph J. Cordes and C. Eugene Steuele, note,

> Under current tax law, capital gains on assets that are transferred at death are effectively exempt from the income tax. The estate tax ensures that at least a portion of those capital gains are taxed in some way. The wealthiest individuals in society seldom recognize more than a tiny portion of their income, hence pay a lower rate of effective individual income tax than many middle-income tax payers.[82]

The complaint that the estate tax is double taxation is a rhetorical point, not an economic principle. There is no a priori economic principle of taxation that articulates that money *should not* be taxed at various junctures as it moves through the economy and that government should not impose taxes on distinct transactions.

Liam Murphy and Thomas Nagel write that the issue is not the number of times an asset has been taxed.

> It is hard to be sure whether the objection [to double taxation] is mere demagoguery or actual confusion. Taxes are not like punishments, which may not be imposed twice for the same crime. Nor is an inheritance tax like a second imposition of the very same income or sales tax on the same earnings or transaction. Multiple distinct taxes often tax people's assets "twice," as when a sales tax is imposed on the expenditure of someone's after-tax income, or a property tax is collected on an asset that was bought with income subject to tax. Any issue of fairness in such cases would have to be about the cumulative effect of multiple taxes, not about double taxation per se.[83]

As a society, we tax transactions, the movement of money through the economy. That's a fundamental element of our tax system. If we disqualified a tax on the basis that somewhere along the chain of transactions another tax was imposed, we would eliminate virtually all taxation. Such an abolition may be a libertarian political objective, but it is not a way to pay for the government services that we all depend upon.

In fact, one of the reasons why an estate tax is fair is because most of these other forms of taxation are highly regressive. A person of modest means will pay taxes on most of his or her transactions—wages, purchases, interest earnings—whereas a wealthy person will pay a disproportionately smaller percentage of his or her income on the same events.

DOES THE ESTATE TAX PENALIZE THE LITTLE GUYS?
One allegation about the estate tax is that it is "voluntary" for the very wealthy, because they can afford to hire planners to enable them to avoid it or significantly reduce its bite. Pro-repeal advocates suggest the tax hits harder for family businesses and less wealthy individuals, who cannot afford expensive tax shelters and

don't have the luxury of liquidity. This is a variation on the Leona Helmsley statement: "Only the little people pay taxes."

It is true that the very wealthy can afford to pay a higher estate tax than less wealthy households. Taxing away 40 percent of a $100 million estate leaves those heirs with significantly more wealth than what remains after a $2 million estate pays 20 percent. That is the whole rationale for progressive taxation—those with the greatest ability to pay, pay more. That is also why we support raising exemptions and maintaining a graduated rate to the estate tax.

But the estate tax is not a voluntary tax for the super wealthy. Examining IRS data from 1999, the latest year for which data are available, we find that over half of the estate tax revenue comes from the 6.6 percent of taxable estates that exceed $5 million. And the wealthiest 467 estates out of the total 49,870 that pay any tax account for 23.8 percent of total estate tax revenues. In 2001, this raised $5.5 billion, or $11.7 million per estate exceeding $20 million.[84]

If the very wealthy could readily avoid the estate tax, why are they spending so much effort and money to repeal it? There are really only three ways to *substantially* avoid the estate tax. First, give it all to your surviving spouse (which postpones the tax until the survivor dies). Second, give it all to charity. Third, spend all your money while you are alive.

There are two primary exemptions, as noted earlier, which are the marital deduction and the charitable deduction. Other ways in which people can reduce their estate tax liabilities are through giving while they are alive and setting up different kinds of trusts. Since this is not a tax-planning primer, we won't go into the minutiae of these mechanisms.[85] But here is how some of them work, from a policy point of view.

Some families use what's called the annual exclusion, which allows inter vivos (between the living) gifts, thereby reducing the size of the estate. Each spouse can give up to eleven thousand dollars every year to every child, grandchild, or any other individual. One analysis found that "roughly one-quarter of the wealth transfers between succeeding generations could be sheltered from transfer taxes" by use of the annual exclusion.[86]

This is not to suggest that people don't exert effort to avoid or reduce estate taxes, but people attempt to avoid every form of taxation, especially the income tax. The impact of these avoidance arrangements, however, is greatly exaggerated.

DOES THE ESTATE TAX RAISE ENOUGH REVENUE
TO COVER THE COST OF COLLECTING IT?
One of the allegations about the estate tax that is a staple of conservative talk radio is the notion that the estate tax costs as much to administer as it raises. Over and over, we encountered this red herring. It is one of many unfortunate examples of how repeal advocates play fast and loose with the facts in the debate over the estate tax.

Here is a brief case study on the anatomy and distribution of a falsehood. First, the allegations: the Center on Taxation and Policy intones on its widely circulated Internet fact sheet that "according to the Joint Economic Committee, the cost equals the tax collected." Its "Reasons the Death Tax Does not Work" argues that the estate tax "collects just one percent of the nation's revenues, and dollar for dollar, it costs as much to collect Death Taxes as it raises."[87]

The *Seattle Times* vigorously publicized the allegation that "it costs the government 65 cents of every dollar raised for enforcement and compliance." This misrepresentation was repeated in many advertisements developed by the *Seattle Times* and was reprinted in other newspapers for millions of readers. Finally, it was repeated by legislators like Representative Jennifer Dunn in the halls of Congress.[88]

There are two different "costs" worth examining in this discussion that have been confused. First, the administrative costs are borne directly by the Internal Revenue Service in operating, monitoring, and enforcing the estate tax. Second, the direct compliance costs are borne by taxpayers in the form of time and money spent on tax advice and implementation of estate-planning arrangements. In this loose debate, the distinctions between these two types of costs have been blurred. You would presume from the allegations that the IRS spends the equivalent amount of money collecting the tax as it raises in revenue. But critics might also be including the total estimated costs of taxpayer compliance, including all the money people spend on lawyers and planners. In some cases, they also include the cost of all the premiums paid on life insurance. Even combining all these factors, the real total doesn't begin to approach the revenue the estate tax raises.

So where did these inaccuracies come from? Repeal advocates quote a study conducted by researcher Alicia Munnell and cited by the Joint Economic Committee. What Munnell actually wrote was that compliance costs "may well approach the revenue yield." Even this more qualified conclusion, however, was based on clearly unwarranted assumptions.[89]

Munnell's estimate is based on an American Bar Association report in which sixteen thousand lawyers cited trust, probate, and estate law as their area of concentration. Munnell estimates that, valuing these lawyers' time at $150,000 a year and assuming they spend half of their billable time on estate tax planning, their work yields $1.2 billion in avoidance costs. Lawyers say this estimate is extravagant.

This $1.2 billion is compared with estate tax revenues of $7.7 billion in 1987. To account for the $6.5 billion gap, Munnell casually adds the estimated cost of "accountants eager to gain an increasing share of the estate planning market." All told, in Munnell's estimates, financial planners and insurance agents who devote time to minimizing estate avoidance costs "must amount to billions of dollars annually."[90] Reckless repeal advocates converted this imprecise guess to a hard figure of something close to $6.5 billion. We are not talking facts here.

Munnell's guesses are now seriously out of date, and estate tax revenues have risen dramatically during the intervening period. The estate tax generated $7.7 billion in 1987, but it generated almost $30 billion in 1999. Compliance costs are a small fraction of the annual collection.[91]

Such was the folly of the debate over the estate tax. A fact about the cost of compliance that was repeated thousands of times was a stretch in 1987 when it was first suggested. Sixteen years later, it is still being repeated without a reasonable basis.

Studies that argue that life insurance premiums should count as a compliance cost are equally far-fetched. Gale and Slemrod point out that "this expense is properly thought of as prepaying the tax liability, and to consider it as a cost in addition to the tax liability itself is surely inappropriate double counting."[92]

So what are the real costs of taxpayer compliance and administration of the estate tax? Several academic studies estimate taxpayer compliance costs at less than 7 percent of revenues—a long way from 100 percent. Charles Davenport and Jay Soled base their estimates on tax-planning costs of $1.047 billion in 1999, plus $628 million for estate administration costs, for a total of $1.675 billion in 1999, or about 6.4 percent of expected receipts.[93]

Many of the costs attributed to estate tax planning would have been paid even without an estate tax. It is difficult to segment tax and financial planning services that are specific to the estate tax compliance with other planning services such as business succession and planning for how heirs will be treated. Business tax expert James Repetti argues that "a significant portion of these costs would be incurred even in the absence of estate taxes."[94] People will still need wills and lawyers and accountants if there is no estate tax.

There are serious costs associated with all taxes. Consider the income tax: folks with large income tax liabilities have substantial costs that are incurred not once or twice in a lifetime but every year. There is no serious effort to repeal the income tax. Further, if estate tax exemptions are raised, the number who may seek professional help in anticipation of paying estate taxes is reduced to a small number of our wealthiest citizens.

As for the costs to the IRS, estimates indicate that the estate tax costs slightly more to administer than other forms of taxation.

This is because of the greater complexity of the tax when audits are involved. University of Michigan researcher Joel Slemrod concludes that collection costs for U.S. individual and corporate income tax are about 10 percent of the revenue collected. The estate tax falls within this estimate.[95] One important fact to remember is that the entire budget for all of the Internal Revenue Service's activities is $8 billion, whereas the estate tax has consistently raised in excess of $28 billion over the last few years.[96]

IS THE TOP RATE OF THE ESTATE TAX TOO HIGH?
Proponents of repeal were very successful in emblazoning the 55 percent top rate into people's minds. In its "talking points" for repeal advocates, the Center on Tax and Policy underscores why it is important to talk about the top rate. "That 55 percent top tax rate is a real home run. You cannot emphasize the 55 percent top rate too often," exhorts the center.

> We already know from the telephone survey we conducted that Americans find the estate tax more unfair than any other levy. But what really ticks Americans off is the 55 percent figure. No American, no matter how rich, should have to give up more than half of their savings when they die. That's simply not the American way.[97]

The fact is that the top rate is no longer 55 percent; it is now 50 percent and will shortly be reduced to 45 percent.

The Center for Taxation and Policy also provides an inaccurate international comparison, stating that "Japan has an inheritance tax of 70%, but after credits and exemptions it is an effective tax rate of 30.3%. The United States has the highest rate of estate tax in the world at the rate of 55% and an effective rate of 44%." (Effective rate is the actual percentage of an estate that is paid, as distinct from the top marginal rate.) This claim is not true on two counts. First, a number of countries have much higher top tax rates on their estate and inheritance taxes.[98] Second, the overall effective rate of the U.S. estate tax in 1999 was 24 percent. According to the IRS, the total value of taxable estates was $84 billion and the tax collected $20 billion. The rate structure was progressive, so a family with a $1.5 million estate paid a significantly lower effective rate than a household with a $100 million estate. The effective rate on estates with assets over $10 million is 37 percent. If proponents continue to argue that households pay effective rates equal to the top marginal rate, they should be asked to identify people for whom this is true.

One of the challenges of explaining tax policy is the complexity of marginal tax rates. The top tax rate was 55 percent for the value of estates over $3 million. So a $4 million estate would pay the top rate only on the $1 million over the $3 million threshold. In the 2001 tax bill that passed, the estate tax rate structure is gradually reduced from 50 percent in 2002 to 45 percent in 2009. This will further reduce the effective rate and progressivity of the tax.

The most important number is not the top rate but the effective rate. An estate tax with fewer exemptions and loopholes could have a lower rate and still generate significant revenue. We stand by the proposition that paying effectively one-quarter to one-third of one's estate at death is a reasonable toll.

HOW MUCH DOES THE ESTATE TAX REALLY RAISE?

> Everybody involved agrees that this tax doesn't raise that much money—$30 billion a year, which is small potatoes, not even a french fry in the federal budget.
>
> —Tucker Carlson[99]

In the partisan hyperbole of federal budget debates, $30 billion could be either an "irrelevant sliver of revenue" or a "bloated appropriation" depending on your point of view. Consider the fireworks that would explode over a $30 billion spending initiative.

First, the estate tax raises a lot of money. In the immortal words attributed to the late Senate minority leader Everett Dirksen, "a billion here, a billion there, and pretty soon you're talking real money."[100] The revenue from the estate tax is more than Washington State's annual budget. It would provide the revenue to rebuild New York City after the terrorist attacks and still have enough left over to pay for the federal budget for the entire Department of Housing and Urban Development. Thirty billion dollars of revenue from a steady and progressive source is nothing to sneeze at.

According to the Center for Budget and Policy Priorities, the estate tax generates 9 percent of all discretionary spending, meaning funds not already earmarked for Social Security, Medicare, and the military. Thirty billion dollars would go a long way toward repairing schools, providing health insurance to children, and providing prescription drug coverage for seniors. Studies that look at the long-term Social Security deficit estimate that it is close to the amount of revenue that will be lost from estate tax repeal.[101]

Second, the estate tax will be a significant source of revenue in the future. As we have said, the wealth expansion of the last generation, albeit diminished by the current recession, is huge. In chapter 1, we discussed the incredible revenue potential that exists from the estate tax. A conservative estimate of the intergenerational transfer of wealth and future estate tax suggests that over the next fifty years the estate tax will generate $171 billion a year from estates valued at over $5 million. Removing this significant source of future revenue would constitute a significant tax burden shift off those most able to pay and onto everyone else.

Finally, it is ironic that the same special interest groups that have weakened the estate tax with special provisions now denigrate its revenue-raising potency. Since its inception in 1916, the revenue-generating abilities of the estate tax have steadily declined. The tax reached its zenith of revenue production in 1936, when it accounted for 11 percent of federal revenues. By 1940, this figure had dropped to 5 percent, then to 2.5 percent in 1965, and finally to 1 percent in 1990. There is no reason that a targeted and simplified estate tax couldn't generate a steady 2 to 5 percent of federal revenue in the future.

CHAPTER FOUR

The Showdown

During the summer of 2000, our country came within a cat's whisker of repealing the estate tax. Congress had passed repeal. Only President Clinton's veto in late August 2000 prevented the change from being enacted.

During the 2000 presidential campaign, most of the GOP candidates made elimination of the "death tax" a cornerstone of their programs. Presidential aspirant Steve Forbes led the battle cry of "no taxation without respiration," a central focus of his tax-slashing candidacy. Candidate George W. Bush, who considered Forbes as a serious rival for the conservative base of the party, also campaigned on the elimination of the estate tax as part of his tax cut proposal.

When George W. Bush was elected president, it was a great day for estate tax repeal proponents. Days after the election was finalized, the *Wall Street Journal* reported "at or near the top of [Bush's tax initiatives] is estate tax relief, an area that has drawn the most attention from Mr. Bush's wealthiest supporters."[1]

Shortly after his inauguration, President Bush announced his $1.6 trillion tax cut proposal. It included estate tax repeal as a central component. The other components of the tax bill included a reduction in all income tax rates, elimination of the "marriage penalty," and the expansion of the child tax credit. The price of the estate tax repeal portion was estimated at $236 billion over ten years, a number that would only increase over the ensuing months.

There were, however, several bumps on the road for repeal forces, mostly related to the fiscal imprudence of the plan. First came Congress's budget agreement framework, which trimmed the scale of the president's tax proposal to $1.35 trillion. Second, economists began to express skepticism about the design of the president's proposal as an economic stimulus in the face of a recession.

Third, the estimated cost of the whole tax cut, and repeal of the estate tax in particular, began to mushroom. Previous estimates of complete estate tax repeal had failed to include the cost implications of the new income tax loopholes that would be created after repeal.

Fourth, proponents of reform (but not repeal) started to get organized and contest the previously unchallenged assertions of repealers. Prior to February 2001, there was very little organized opposition to wholesale repeal. But as the cherry blossoms in D.C. started to bloom, there was a rumbling in the land.

BUDGET FRAMEWORK

In order to understand how we ended up with the 2001 tax cut, let's take a look at the federal budgeting process. As part of this process, Congress establishes a so-called budget resolution framework. The budget resolution aims to do two things: (1) set spending targets for each of the thirteen annual appropriations bills; (2) establish the provisions and procedures to package and streamline the passage of tax- and spending-related legislation. Although not a public law, the budget resolution is initiated by House and Senate budget committees and passed in both houses. It then goes to a conference committee, and any compromise is passed in both houses. Unlike an actual law, it does not go to the White House, and the administration has no formal role in setting the framework.[2]

The budget resolution for the 2001 tax cut was probably the

largest tax cut ever passed through the budget reconciliation process. But it could have been even bigger. A number of Republican and Democratic moderates, out of concern for the fiscal impact of the tax cut proposal, reduced the amount of the budget available for tax cuts.

Since the budget-writing process moves on a fast track, Congress has adopted protections to ensure that budget bills don't get laden down with hundreds of extraneous amendments and provisions. Some rules are specific to maintaining fiscal discipline.

One of the budget-writing rules, adopted in 1986, is known as the Byrd Rule, named after Senator Robert Byrd of West Virginia. The intention of this provision is to prevent commitments that create budget deficits in outlying years. The Byrd Rule excludes amendments that would have spending or revenue implications beyond the ten-year budget-planning window. In the Senate, suspension of the Byrd Rule requires sixty votes. Proponents of repeal have not been able to obtain these sixty votes.

Because the estate tax repeal provision has long-term implications for federal revenue, the Byrd Rule is the reason why the estate tax repeal sunsets at the end of 2010 as if the 2001 tax cut never existed. Without this rule imposing fiscal responsibility, complete estate tax repeal would have been permanent.

The president's overall tax cut was marketed to the American public on two main points: (1) There was a massive surplus of $5.6 trillion; therefore we should return $1.6 trillion in taxpayer's money, and (2) the tax cut will help the economy as it slips into recession.

Shortly after the release of the president's tax cut proposal, a number of economists, political leaders and commentators began to question some of the "fuzzy math" and economic assumptions behind the tax cut. Economists pointed out that if the estimated near-term Social Security surplus was subtracted from the rosy projection of a $5.6 trillion surplus over ten years, it would leave approximately $2.4 to $3 trillion of surplus.[3] Setting aside near-term Medicare surpluses and using more prudent and realistic assumptions about tax increases and program reductions left a sum of $1.5 to $2 trillion over ten years, about the amount of the entire proposed tax cut.[4]

Given the president's campaign pledges to expand education and prescription drug coverage, many observers wondered aloud where the money would come from. Deficit hawks from the Concord Coalition issued a statement of concern, signed by coalition cochairs former senators Warren Rudman (R-N.H.) and Sam Nunn (D-Ga.), along with former treasury secretary Robert Rubin, former Federal Reserve chairman Paul Volcker, and former secretary of commerce in the Nixon administration Pete Peterson. As to whether tax cuts should be based on the ten-year projections of the Congressional Budget Office, the Concord Coalition leaders responded, "it would be exceedingly unwise to rely on these projections to lock in a series of large, escalating tax cuts, particularly before addressing the implications of the future financing requirements of Social Security and Medicare."[5] They advocated for a modest two- or three-year tax reduction and then a reassessment about the prudence of additional tax cuts.

The tax cut was urgently marketed as help for the emerging recession. But the Bush tax proposal was in fact not designed to stimulate the economy. Even Bush's own treasury secretary, Paul O'Neil, in a January 17 confirmation hearing before the Senate Finance Committee, expressed doubts about the value of tax cuts as a potent fiscal stimulus.[6] Economists gathering at the January 2001 meeting of the American Economic Association were in agreement in their skepticism about the efficacy of tax cuts as a short-term economic stimulus. As a *Wall Street Journal* article about the gathering reported, there was "a rare consensus" among the economists "that monetary policy—the adjusting of short-term interest rates by the Federal Reserve—is the first and best way to ward off recession. Priming the economic pump with fiscal stimulus, either government spending or lower taxes, is said to be an inefficient way to get the job done."[7]

Among the components of the tax package, the estate tax was

viewed by economists as having the least stimulus impact.[8] As several economists pointed out, the Bush tax plan was designed in 1999, during a booming economy, as a political foil against candidate Steve Forbes.[9] Virtually none of its provisions were aimed at providing short-term economic stimulus. This would prove to be the beginning of a multiyear debate as to what would constitute an "economic stimulus."

By March, as the economy started to slow and stock market indexes tumbled, pressure mounted for a tax cut that would take place immediately. As a result, some legislators pushed a proposal to reduce the lowest tax bracket and rush a rebate to all taxpayers. But the Bush administration and conservative tax writers understood the peril of unlinking the popular rebate proposal from the rest of the package and worked to keep it together.[10] If ordinary Americans were going to get their tax rebate, they would have to cut the top tax rate and repeal the estate tax too.

As time went on, it was clear that the top rate cut and the estate tax repeal were the sacred cows of the tax cut. Other provisions of the tax cut, such as eliminating the marriage penalty and lowering bottom tax rates were merely pretty packaging to win over popular support. The *Wall Street Journal* reported that Republican leaders were concerned that the "across-the-board" tax cut was skewed too much toward lower- and middle-income taxpayers.[11] Even the cost of the packaging was too high for some.

Enthusiasm for reducing the top tax rate led on occasion to effusive exaggeration. President Bush on the stump exclaimed that "nationwide there are more than 17.4 million small-business owners and entrepreneurs who stand to benefit" from the top rate reduction.[12] But a study by the Institute for Taxation and Economic Policy showed that in 1999 only about 800,000 taxpayers paid the top rate, and only 160,000 of those were self-employed.[13]

A year later, in the spring of 2002, it became clear where the real priorities lay. In negotiating with the new Democratic Senate majority over what provision of the tax bill to make permanent first, conservative leaders pushed the estate tax repeal provision.

Only later would they pledge to make other sections of the tax cut permanent, like the elimination of the marriage penalty. The provisions that benefited their wealthy contributors would be the first priority.

FISCAL RESPONSIBILITY AND THE RISING COSTS OF ESTATE TAX REPEAL

Estate tax repeal was always recognized to be an expensive and regressive component of the overall tax package. The president's 2001 proposal was to repeal the estate tax over ten years. But in the tenth year, repeal would account for nearly 25 percent of the lost revenue of the entire tax cut package. Initial estimates showed that repeal would cost less than $250 billion over the first ten years, but in the second decade the cost of repeal would explode to $750 billion.[14]

The first evidence that the estate tax repeal part of the tax plan might be in trouble began to emerge in late January 2001. An article in the *New York Times*, "Some Experts Questioning Bush Plan on Estate Taxes," reported that the real cost of repeal would vastly exceed the January estimate of $236 billion over ten years.[15] A number of tax experts, including Jonathan Blattmachr of Milbank, Tweed, Hadley & McCloy in New York, expressed concern that repeal would open up unanticipated loopholes. For instance, repealing the gift tax would encourage income tax avoidance by wealthy individuals through large-scale gift transfers, shifting ownership to relatives in no-tax states and other manipulations. One avoidance scenario was described as follows:

> Consider, for one, the case of an individual with stock that has grown in value by $100 million. Currently, if the stockholder sold, she would owe $20 million in capital gains taxes. If she gave the stock to a relative, she would have to pay $55 million in gift taxes, and if the relative sold the stock, he would owe $9 million capital gains. But if the gift and estate taxes were repealed without conditions, a family maneuver could permit the stock to be sold and the full $100 million in profit realized without payment of any capital gains tax. Here is

how: The owner would give the stock to an older relative—say an
uncle—who is expected to live at least a year. The uncle would leave
the stock to his niece, the original owner, in his will. When the uncle
died, the stock would be returned to the niece at its new value, tax
free.[16]

Some experts criticized the tax-writing committee staff for not
factoring in all of the creative avoidance mechanisms that would
crop up.[17]

Indeed, the congressional Joint Tax Committee began to assess the dynamic interaction between estate tax repeal and income
tax avoidance. Committee members delayed the release of these
estimates, at the behest of pro-repeal legislators, in order to post-
pone the political fallout. But finally Charles Rangel, ranking
Democratic member of the House Ways and Means Committee,
forced the Joint Tax Committee to reveal the new estimates that
proved devastating to the repeal cause.

The bipartisan Joint Tax Committee found that proposals to
eliminate the estate and gift taxes would open, as anticipated, new
loopholes and income tax avoidance schemes. The estimated cost
rose to $662.2 billion over ten years, more than double the previ-
ous estimates. New loopholes alone accounted for $252 billion of
the previously unanticipated costs, largely in lost income tax revenue.[18] Estimated losses for the second ten years were over $800 bil-
lion. The cut, in other words, was very back-end loaded in terms
of cost.

These estimates, combined with organized opposition, caused
pro-repeal forces to stumble. The *Wall Street Journal* noted that
these revised estimates raised "further uncertainty over already-
embattled efforts to ease the tax."[19] The House Ways and Means
tax-writing committee set out to shoehorn the repeal of the estate
tax repeal into a scaled-back tax package along with the more politically popular provisions such as elimination of the marriage
penalty and income tax rate reductions. This was accomplished
by including a long phaseout and delayed effective date. In the
end, this deliberately masked the real long-term costs of estate
tax repeal.

ORGANIZING TO OPPOSE COMPLETE REPEAL

When asked in the spring of 2000 if there was any one group or individual dedicated to preserving the tax, Joel Slemrod, director of the Office of Tax Policy Research at the University of Michigan Business School, haltingly told a reporter, "Al . . . Gore."[20] This was an honest reflection, at the time, of the absence of organized defenders of the estate tax.

Starting in January and February 2001, a number of coalitions emerged to oppose all or different aspects of the Bush tax proposal. The Fair Taxes for All coalition, a national alliance of five hundred organizations convened by People for the American Way and the American Federation of State, County, and Municipal Employees, came together to oppose the scale and priorities of the entire tax cut.

Several ad hoc groups formed to oppose estate tax repeal. Nonprofits to Preserve the Estate Tax (later renamed Americans for a Fair Estate Tax) was convened by the Washington-based OMB Watch to mobilize charities and nonprofit organizations that would be adversely affected by the impact of repeal on charitable giving.

Previous debates about the estate tax had not included the impact of repeal on charitable giving. But one high-level defector from the repeal camp underscored this point. In an interview with the *New York Times,* John DiIulio Jr., the first director of President Bush's Office on Faith-Based and Community Initiatives, expressed his opposition to repeal. Concerned about the adverse impact of estate tax repeal on religious charities, DiIulio told an interviewer, "I don't want to be the skunk at the picnic, but no, I don't think the estate tax should be eliminated—modified, maybe, but not eliminated."[21]

It appeared that the president's two policy proposals—faith-based initiatives and estate tax repeal—might potentially work against each other. One initiative would mobilize government support to religious organizations performing needed services, while the other would undercut charitable gifts and bequests to religious organizations.

Responsible Wealth was part of this coalition concerned about charities and also spoke to the dangers of concentrated wealth and power. Responsible Wealth is a project of the Boston-based United for a Fair Economy, which was founded in 1995 with a concern about wealth and income inequality. Responsible Wealth mobilized business leaders and high-net-worth investors to oppose public policies that would worsen inequality.

United for a Fair Economy and Responsible Wealth had opposed repeal of the estate tax during the summer of 2000 when they pulled together an eleventh-hour effort to ensure that the House would have enough votes to uphold President Clinton's veto and preserve the tax. They purchased advertisements and enlisted a number of national organizations to issue statements. But because most constituency groups were confident that President Clinton would veto tax repeal legislation, it was difficult to mobilize organizations to defend it.[22]

These coalitions supported estate tax reform, but not repeal. They underscored the fundamental unfairness of estate tax repeal and the lopsided distribution of tax benefits. One study by the Center on Budget and Policy Priorities noted that forty-five hundred of the largest estates would receive as much tax relief from the Bush tax plan as 142 million Americans combined.[23]

Another alliance formed to oppose the repeal of the estate tax was the Americans for Sensible Estate Tax Solutions (ASSETS), a coalition formed by the Association for Advanced Life Underwriting and the National Association of Insurance and Financial Advisors. ASSETS enlisted a Wyoming Republican, former senator Alan Simpson, as its lead spokesperson. In testimony he submitted to the Senate Finance Committee, he talked about the experience he and his wife, Ann, had in serving on the boards of charitable institutions, including the Folger Shakespeare Library, the Buffalo Bill Historical Center, and the Kennedy Center. "I have seen first hand how the estate tax promotes charitable giving."[24]

Simpson and the ASSETS coalition advocated for immediate reforms to raise exemptions rather than waiting ten years for a phaseout. Their proposal was to exempt 84 percent of the nearly fifty thousand estates currently subject to the tax, while maintaining it on approximately the richest six thousand estates.[25]

One concern that ASSETS brought to the debate was how longer-term reform made it difficult for people to obtain tax advice with any certainty. "The phase out of the estate tax depends too much on what a future Congress may or may not do," stated Simpson in his testimony. The Bush proposal enabled the 107th Congress to "make a politically expedient promise that the members of the 111th Congress will be expected to carry out." Former senator Simpson seemed to predict the future in his testimony.

> To enact legislation on the assumption that an "estate tax repeal" won't be modified or reinstated by a future Congress simply assumes too much. Now as I don my Republican hat, I would like the members of this distinguished panel, particularly the current majority, to assume the possibility . . . however frightening you think it may be! . . . that 1) the control of Congress shifts and 2) a future Congress may need additional revenues in order to fund some disaster relief.[26]

Simpson's testimony was prescient in light of the quick shift in party control in the Senate in June 2001 and the fiscal impact of the September 11 terrorist attacks and recession.

Throughout January and early February, Responsible Wealth drafted its Call to Preserve the Estate Tax and quietly enlisted signers. When it had enlisted one hundred initial signers, it reserved several newspaper advertisements to publicize its statement. On Valentine's Day, 2001, a story about the effort broke with a front-page article in the *New York Times* and the *International Herald Tribune.* "Dozens of Rich Americans Join in Fight to Retain the Estate Tax," proclaimed the headline. "Buffett, Soros and Gates' Father Call It Only Fair."

Warren Buffett told Pulitzer Prize-winning reporter David Cay Johnston that repealing the estate tax "would be a terrible mistake," comparable to "choosing the 2020 Olympic team by picking the eldest sons of the gold-medal winners in the 2000 Olympics." "We have come closer to a true meritocracy than anywhere else around the world," Buffett continued. "You have mobility, so people with talents can be put to the best use. Without the estate tax, you in effect will have an aristocracy of wealth, which means you pass down the ability to command the resources of the nation based on heredity rather than merit."[27] Salon.com pointed out the irony that this "most stirring defense of the progressive tax system, and American meritocracy, should come from the world's fourth wealthiest man. Maybe," they speculated, "that will insulate him from charges of class warfare."[28]

That day, Responsible Wealth was contacted by over one hundred major news media outlets. Its signers and spokespeople conducted dozens of major television interviews. Thanks to an otherwise slack news week, the story propelled forward for several more days, with impressive editorial page support.

Responsible Wealth took out an ad in the *New York Times*. The lead signers included Rockefeller family members Steven C. Rockefeller, Eileen Rockefeller Growald, and David Rockefeller Jr.; financier George Soros; art patron Agnes Gund; and philanthropists Henry and Edith Everett. Also included were telecommunications company founder Peter Barnes; former Stanford University provost Richard Lyman and his wife, Jing; George and Jane Russell; Professor Frank Roosevelt; actor Paul Newman; and more than two hundred others.

In the days and weeks after the ad appeared, the signers of Responsible Wealth's Call to Preserve the Estate Tax were joined by venture capitalist and founder of Tiger Fund Julian Robertson, chief operating engineer of Sun Microsystems Bill Joy, author Annie Dillard, vice chairman of AOL–Time Warner Ted Turner, television producer Norman Lear, developer of PageMaker Paul Brainard, renowned venture capitalist of Rock Associates Arthur Rock, and retired chairman of American Airlines Robert Crandall. The signers included Democrats, Republicans, and Independents, a group not easy to pigeonhole.

Although the news media focused on the well-known names and mischaracterized the group as "billionaires" (there were only four billionaires in the original mix), many of the signers were

small business owners and individuals with estates valued below
$10 million.

Throughout the spring of 2001, a real debate about the estate
tax began. Though it was clouded with myths about who would
benefit from repeal, there was growing public understanding of
some of the positive aspects of retaining the tax. Unfortunately,
many members of Congress had already pledged their vote to the
repeal side.

THE ESTATE TAX: A SUMMARY OF CHANGES

Congress could have done one of three things in regard to the estate tax. It could have left the tax as it was, reformed it, or completely repealed it. In the end, it did all three.[29] On May 26, 2001,
Congress passed the Bush tax bill, technically titled "The Economic Growth and Tax Relief Reconciliation Act of 2001."
Support for the overall tax bill was considerable. It passed the
House of Representatives by a vote of 240 to 154, with twenty-
eight Democrats and one independent joining all of the Republicans in voting yes. The Senate approved the bill by a margin of
fifty-eight to thirty-three, with twelve Democrats joining forty-
six Republicans in support. Only two Republicans, Senator John
McCain (R-Ariz.) and Senator Lincoln Chaffee (R-R. I.), voted
against the bill.

The immediate reviews for the tax cut were overwhelmingly
negative. Money guru Jane Bryant Quinn called it "a contempt-
ible piece of consumer fraud."[30] One group of respected budget
analysts concluded that the 2001 tax bill "appears to contain more
budget gimmicks than any tax bill—and quite possibly any piece
of major legislation—in recent history."[31]

The main criticism of the overall tax bill is that it wedges too
many expensive features into a limited framework. The tax cut
could not exceed the $1.35 trillion framework established as part
of the budget process. Yet the estate tax repeal alone, once fully
phased in, would cost $850 billion over ten years.

As a result, the tax bill has a bizarre assortment of phase-ins,
phaseouts, and delayed starts. It then culminates with a complete

sunset of the bill at the end of 2010, when federal tax law reverts back to what it was in May 2001. In one example of budget contortions, the tax bill delays $33 billion in corporate tax receipts by two weeks, shifting the revenue from fiscal year 2001, which was outside the budget window, to fiscal year 2002, which is inside the budget window. As William Gale and Samara Potter note, "the sole purpose was to increase funds available to finance tax cuts in the 2002–2011 budget window even though there was no underlying improvement in government finances."[32]

The bill greatly favors the very wealthy, allocating 38 percent of the plan's tax cuts to the best-off 1.3 million of all taxpayers, while sharing less than 15 percent of the tax breaks with the 78 million individuals and families in the bottom three-fifths of the income scale.[33] The estate tax repeal is the single greatest factor in the regressivity of the bill. According to Citizens for Tax Justice, the real cost of the total tax cut—factoring in extra interest payments, maintaining expiring provisions, and fixing the Alternative Minimum Tax—will be $2.2 trillion over ten years.[34] The cost of the tax bill, if it were to survive a second decade, would be $4.1 trillion over the ten-year period 2011 to 2022.[35]

The long-term effect of the 2001 tax bill is a fiscal train wreck. Social Security and Medicare face substantial deficits over the next seventy-five years and beyond. Future budget projects show a significant budget gap in outlying decades, even without the 2001 tax cut. With the tax cut, however, the fiscal gap is tripled over the next seventy-five years.[36]

The amount of wealth exempted by the estate tax rises between 2002 and 2009 and the top rate declines. Then, on January 1, 2010, the estate tax is completely repealed. The gift tax is not repealed, to prevent the income tax avoidance schemes described earlier in the chapter. The main changes in the estate tax include the following:

The decline of top rates. The highest estate and gift tax rate drops from 55 percent to 45 percent by 2007. Under the bill, effective January 1, 2002, the 5 percent surtax (which phases out the benefit of the graduated rates), and all estate and gift tax rates in excess of

50 percent, were repealed. Every year between 2003 and 2007 the rate drops one percentage point.

The increase in wealth exemptions. In 2002, the unified credit effective exemption amount (for both estate and gift tax purposes) rose from $675,000 to $1 million. It subsequently rises in stages to $3.5 million by 2009, the year before full repeal. These exemption figures are doubled for couples.

The elimination of family business advantages. In 2004, the qualified family-owned business deduction currently provided is repealed.[37] This is an interesting change and an abandonment of the notion of a special status for family business. Once again, this was likely a cost consideration, but it may also have been a recognition of the problems in defining a qualified family-owned business.

The change in gift tax rates. In 2010, all estate and generation-skipping transfer taxes will be repealed. A gift tax, however, will remain in effect at a rate equal to the top individual income tax rate (subject to a lifetime $1 million exemption amount).

The phaseout of the state tax credit by 2005. In 2002, the state tax credit is reduced by 25 percent; in 2003 by 50 percent; in 2004 by 75 percent. It is completely phased out by 2005. If payment is made for a state inheritance or estate tax liability, that amount can be deducted against the federal tax. As we discussed earlier, this will have a serious negative impact on state revenues.

The modification of carryover basis. After complete repeal in 2010, a modified "carryover basis" for property acquired from a decedent is implemented. Only after estate and generation-skipping transfer taxes have been completely repealed will there be an elimination of "stepped-up" basis at death. Prior to 2010, the estate tax is assessed on the fair market value of assets at death, and heirs may use those stepped-up values as their cost basis when the inherited property is sold.

Under the 2001 estate tax repeal law, the estate tax is replaced by a capital gains tax on the appreciated value of an asset from its original cost rather than from its value at the time of death, when the property is sold. This change will require very complicated record keeping and reporting requirements. As we have seen, after such a provision was passed by Congress in 1976 it was repealed because of its complexity and strong opposition by wealthy interests.[38]

Even if the "carryover basis" provision is ultimately implemented, it would lead to a substantial decline in revenue. A Congressional Budget Office analysis of carryover basis found that it would raise significantly less than 12 percent of the revenue lost to estate tax repeal.[39]

A number of other provisions dealt with matters such as conservation easements.[40] Two other changes were aimed at assisting family enterprises. Starting in 2002, the limit on the number of shareholders eligible for installment payments of the estate tax was increased from fifteen to forty-five, allowing more broadly owned businesses and farm operations to benefit from paying estate tax liability on an installment plan. Also starting in 2002, eligibility for special treatment as a family farm or business was expanded to include lending and finance businesses. Both of these provisions, however, are repealed in 2005, a puzzling provision.

Although some minor components of the 2001 tax law make sense, overall it is bad tax policy—and that's the friendly review. "It's a flimflam," said lawyer William Zabel of Schulte Roth & Zabel in New York.[41] "Laughter is the right response," observed Jane Bryant Quinn. "What are the incentives here?" Quinn asks.

> (1) The "poor rich" ($3.5 million or $7 million) will make fewer gifts. (2) Rich husbands will leave more to their kids and less to trusts that cover their wives. (3) Charities will get stiffed. (4) The rich-rich and their lawyers will get the capital-gains tax on inherited property repealed. (5) In 2010, ailing parents will keep their bedroom doors locked when their children are in the house. It's going to be a great year to die.[42]

Economist Paul Krugman, who called the entire tax bill "a joke" and "absurd by design," offered his most scathing criticism for the estate tax repeal provisions in a column ironically titled "Bad Heir Day":

So in the law as now written, heirs to great wealth face the following situation: If your ailing mother passes away on Dec. 30, 2010, you inherit her estate tax-free. But if she makes it to Jan. 1, 2011, half the estate will be taxed away. That creates some interesting incentives. Maybe they should have called it the Throw Momma From the Train Act of 2001.[43]

Consider the planning nightmares resulting from these changes in the law. At the time the estate tax is repealed, the step-up basis provisions are repealed and replaced with basis carryover rules. Twelve months later, the estate tax is reinstated as if the 2001 tax bill never happened, carryover basis is repealed, and step-up basis is reinstated.

It is no surprise that the advocates for wholesale repeal were not popping their champagne bottles. Patricia Soldano, writing to her supporters shortly after the passage of the tax bill, wrote:

> Now the not-so-good news: While the estate tax and the generation-skipping tax are fully repealed in 2010, the gift tax is not. . . . Instead, after 2010, individuals will have only a $1 million exemption from the gift tax (the gift tax is reduced to the top income tax rate). In addition, a modified carryover basis regime is enacted for 2010. No longer will a decedent's assets receive a basis of the fair market value on the date of death for purposes of calculating the capital gains tax.[44]

It is interesting to note that the most extreme proponents of repeal like Soldano advocate for maintaining "stepped-up" basis at death even without the estate tax. This windfall for the very wealthy was even too expensive and irresponsible for conservative lawmakers, who felt the need to at least resuscitate the discredited capital gains "carryover" proposal.

Proponents of repeal were alarmed by the possibility that the law could revert to pre-2001 tax cut rules. Within weeks of passage, hard core repeal advocates in Washington, D.C., were wearing buttons to "sunset the sunset." Several bills were introduced to accelerate repeal.

Within days of the devastating terrorist attacks of September

11, one senator shockingly testified that as part of the economic stimulus package Congress should immediately repeal the estate tax. The estate tax, second only to the terrorist threat, was what stood in the way of sustained economic prosperity.

In fact, the opposite is true. The tax should be revisited because of how the budgetary needs of the country have changed since September 11, 2001. During times of war, the United States has historically "conscripted wealth" to pay for the increased burdens on the entire society."[45] For these reasons, the current law will not stand. It will have to be changed sometime prior to 2010 when it sunsets.

This fact was not lost on repeal partisans, who brought legislation forward in June 2002 to make the estate repeal permanent. The House easily passed the provision, but the proposal was stopped in the Senate, falling short of the sixty votes needed to win. Over twenty House members and three senators who had originally supported repeal cited the nation's changed fiscal situation as the reason for changing their antirepeal vote.

Future votes lie ahead, and repeal forces will continue to exhort their partisans to keep up the fight. And defenders of reforming the estate tax do not rest either.

CHAPTER FIVE

What We Owe Our Society

Central to the American experiment has been the effort to balance the values of economic liberty with social equity. This is all well and good, but when it comes to estate tax, things get quite personal.

For some, paying the estate tax is an affront to their achievements. After a lifetime of labors, a seemingly distant government has now come to collect. At the moment that the check is being written, some beneficiaries might contemplate the hard work and thrift of the deceased in contrast with some glaring example of government extravagance and waste. It is no wonder that the payment of the estate tax sometimes evokes such bitterness.

How can we justify this tax? At the core of our advocacy for a highly progressive estate tax is our belief that society has a just claim on the accumulated wealth of its most prosperous citizens. This is not rooted in a belief in enforced charity or redistribution, but in an assessment of the undervalued role of society's investment in each of us. This investment is substantial and often invisible.

This is not an easy discussion to have in the United States. It cuts against the grain of our ethos of individual achievement and free enterprise. Yet it goes to the heart of the rationale for the estate tax.

It is important to recognize and even celebrate the role of the individual in the creation of wealth. There is no question that a significant reason some people accumulate great wealth is through their hard work, intelligence, creativity, faithfulness, and sacrifice. Individuals do make a difference, the difference between success and failure. The Chicago Bulls were a hugely different basketball team with Michael Jordan than without him.

Many individuals who accumulate wealth have been thrifty while others may have been profligate. They have worked and saved when others have played and consumed. And they have taken real risks. They have bet the farm or mortgaged the house for a dream. They have put their time, treasures, and talents on the line.

For people who lead large-scale enterprises, we know that leadership makes a difference. Effective leadership of a large corporation or institution can infuse it with greater productivity. Leadership can sometimes be thankless and lonely, and the stresses involved must seem, on many days, more trouble than they are worth.

Individual imagination can make a difference. A creative idea, springing unbidden from one's mind, can reroute the labor of a thousand toilers in a more effective and efficient direction. The wheel, the cotton gin, or the computer chip—some were technological advances in which individual inventors played a decisive role. Or consider how a piece of art, a song, or an evocative gesture on stage and screen can move our hearts in a way nothing else can. We need these individuals and would be impoverished without their gifts to the world. They should be rewarded for their efforts with social recognition and material benefit.

At the same time, it is important to acknowledge the role of a number of influential factors, such as luck, privilege, other people's efforts, and society's investment in the creation of individual wealth. By luck, we mean the good fortune of timing, of benefiting from circumstances beyond any human control. For a religious person, this might be considered God's grace. We all know the experience of bad luck and good luck. In the creation of wealth, it can sometimes be directly linked.

Privilege is the head start that comes to someone by virtue of upbringing. This could mean the social privileges of skin color, which unfortunately still confer too many advantages in our society. It could be the advantages of being born or adopted into a family with social networks, business experience, or inherited wealth.

By other people's efforts, we mean that despite our individual gifts, nothing we do is ours alone. Ideas, products, and books do not emerge in a vacuum—and other people's input, labors, feedback, and suggestions are always involved. As President Franklin D. Roosevelt remarked, "Wealth in the modern world resulted from a combination of individual efforts. In spite of the great importance in our national life of the . . . ingenuity of unusual individuals, the people in the mass have inevitably helped to make large fortunes possible."[1] Unfortunately, the contribution of the team, the helper, the editor, the laborer are often undervalued in measuring wealth and achievement.

Almost a third of the Forbes 400 were born onto the list (149 members in 2001 with an average net worth of $2.6 billion). To use a baseball analogy, they essentially were born rounding third base. And at least another quarter were born well along the base path—meaning they were fortunate enough to inherit a small business, a piece of land with oil under it, or an investment of "parental equity" on flexible terms.[2] They inherited this legacy, combined it with their own skill and effort, and built it into a successful enterprise. They contributed something unique, but they had a significant boost that someone born in the batter's box doesn't have.

In American culture, we are more inclined to enshrine individual success and undervalue society's role in wealth building. But for the good of the country, we need to better account for the origins of wealth and success. This goes beyond the discussion of the estate tax, to how we think about ourselves, as individuals and as a society.

The dominant view about wealth building and success in our culture can be characterized as the "great man" theory of wealth creation. Like the "great man" theory of history, it borders on mythology. Many of us learned in high school history that President Abraham Lincoln "freed the slaves." Yes, Lincoln was a leader and signed the Emancipation Proclamation. But many people were involved in bringing an end to the institution of slavery, including enslaved people themselves, who resisted and pressed their case, along with abolitionists and religious leaders. The "great man" theory usually captures a piece of the truth but greatly oversimplifies it.

Our society is particularly enamored with the "great man" theory of wealth creation. Its folklore fills the pages of our business magazines. In a recent interview, the chief of a global corporation was asked to justify his enormous compensation package. He responded, "I created about $37 billion in shareholder value." The operative word here is "I." There was no mention of the share of wealth created by the company's other 180,000 employees.[3]

You can hear this creed in the voices of individual achievers: "I did it all myself." "I built this fortune myself." "I'm a self-made man." Turn on any libertarian talk radio show and discuss taxes and you will hear such modern bootstrap sagas. These testimonials evoke the image of a cowboy, riding alone out on the range, with money raining down upon him. The problem with this individualistic way of assessing one's own contribution is that it is inaccurate and dishonest.

From this creed of individual achievement, it is a short distance to "I made this money myself" and "It's all mine" and "government has no business taking any part of it." If one really believes that "I did it all myself," then ipso facto any form of taxation is a form of larceny.

The fact that this is the dominant creed in our culture makes it all the more refreshing and unusual when someone breaks out of the mold and offers a different account of his or her success. One of the leaders of the movement to preserve the estate tax is a New York–based software designer named Martin Rothenberg, who has shared his story to underscore his support for reform, rather than repeal, of the estate tax.

I'm a small business owner, and my family is in the top 2 percent of wealthy Americans who would get a windfall if the estate tax is eliminated. But I believe the estate tax should be fixed, not repealed.

Here's why: My wealth is not only a product of my own hard work. It also resulted from a strong economy and lots of public investment in me and others.

I received a good public school education and used free libraries and museums paid for by others. I went to college under the GI Bill. I went to graduate school to study computers and language on a complete government scholarship, paid for by others. While teaching at Syracuse University for twenty-five years, my research was supported by numerous government grants—again, paid for by others.

My university research provided the basis for Syracuse Language Systems, a company I formed in 1991 with some graduate students and my son, Larry. I sold the company in 1998 and then started a new company, Glottal Enterprises. These companies have benefited from the technology-driven economic expansion—a boom fueled by continual public and private investment.

I've never once heard my family complain about the prospect of part of their inheritance going toward an estate tax. That's because we all believe that paying the estate tax does not mean choosing between taking care of your children and giving back to society. You can do both.

I was able to provide well for my family, and, upon my death, I hope taxes on my estate will help fund the kind of programs that benefited me and others from humble backgrounds—a good education, money for research, and targeted investments in poor communities—to help bring opportunity to all Americans.

I believe exemption levels should be raised to better protect farmers and small business owners. But total repeal would undercut equality of opportunity in America. I urge Congress to fix the estate tax, not repeal it.

Martin's biography includes a number of examples of direct public investment, in the form of access to quality public education and scholarships for higher education. Many in the post–World War II generation benefited from low-cost college education and low-interest housing and business loans as tickets onto the wealth-building train.

Yet even for people who didn't gain from such explicit or direct investments, like Rothenberg's publicly funded education, our society makes many investments that are largely invisible and that we take for granted. We would all benefit from a more accurate accounting of the public's investment.

Conrad Hilton, the founder of the vast hotel chain, pointed out in his will that peace is a boon to hotel owners. Consider the fortunes that have been made in the travel and hospitality industry, the cruise ships, resorts, restaurants, and fashionable destinations. After September 11, 2001, all these sectors of the economy were shaken, a powerful illustration of Hilton's point. Without vast taxpayer investments in keeping the peace, as well as in building mundane facilities such as roads and airports, Hilton's fortune would have been much smaller. Many modern billionaires owe much of their wealth to the taxpayers for investing in education and the scientific advancements upon which their products depend.[4]

Warren Buffet, the founder of Berkshire Hathaway, acknowledges this fertile soil when he imagines trying to create wealth in another society. At the 1996 Berkshire Hathaway annual meeting, Buffett noted that the American system "provides me with enormous rewards for what I bring to this society."[5] In a television interview, Buffett stated,

> I personally think that society is responsible for a very significant percentage of what I've earned. If you stick me down in the middle of Bangladesh or Peru or someplace, you'll find out how much this talent is going to produce in the wrong kind of soil. I will be struggling 30 years later. I work in a market system that happens to reward what I do very well—disproportionately well.[6]

For people who have amassed wealth in private enterprise or the stock market, it is important to measure society's contribution to these institutions. We have a regulated marketplace. Our society has created a framework of property law that enables individuals to own and sell property. These socially created systems are greatly undervalued in our history—as well as in our individual assessments of how people accumulate wealth. As Americans, we benefit enormously from two hundred years of property definition and law.

Our legal framework gives status to private property through mechanisms such as real estate titles, stock ownership structures, and other representations of ownership. These mechanisms, which are most fully evolved in the United States and Europe, not only provide security of ownership for the holder but also enable these assets to be leveraged as capital.

Peruvian economist Hernando deSoto describes the invisible power of defined and centralized property systems as essential to unlocking the "mystery of capital." He argues that the key reason for the enormous prosperity gulf between countries like the United States and nations of the southern hemisphere can be attributed to differences in private property titling systems.[7]

The authors have both had the benefit of traveling in Africa, South Asia, and Latin America and have personally seen the tremendous problems facing half of humanity as they struggle for dignity, a healthy environment, and the tools of economic opportunity. We know that it is not for lack of effort and industriousness that these societies struggle.

DeSoto points out that the masses of people living in poverty in former communist countries and nations in the southern hemisphere work primarily in the informal and extralegal sectors of the economy. In some cases, people who might be considered poor by U.S. standards have substantial assets, but because assets lack legal protection and transactions cannot be readily enforced, they cannot unlock the capital within. These assets are what deSoto calls "dead capital." As a result, capital formation cannot effectively occur in countries with highly informal and extralegal property systems.

Prior to 1800, the United States was burdened by the same characteristics that we associate with "developing" and "poor" countries today. But thanks to over two hundred years of effort and public investment, we have built a reliable and sophisticated market system in which personal wealth is not only protected but readily convertible by sale and borrowing to different forms of assets. It is this market system that puts the "worth" in net worth.

The U.S. framework of laws, networks, titles, and transferable property helps facilitate the creation of wealth. The system itself is a form of social wealth, and it is hard to imagine what life would be like without it. DeSoto offers this picture:

> Imagine a country where nobody can identify who owns what, addresses cannot be easily verified, people cannot be made to pay their debts, resources cannot be divided into shares, descriptions of assets are not standardized and cannot be easily compared, and rules that govern property vary from neighborhood to neighborhood or even from street to street. You have just put yourself into the life of a developing country or former communist nation; more precisely, you have imagined life for 80 percent of [the world's] population.[8]

DeSoto believes that no entrepreneur in the West "could be successful without property rights systems based on a strong, well-integrated social contract." This is a vivid reminder of how much of our system of wealth building has been built by the common effort of our ancestors.

We have gone from integrated title systems for real estate to highly complicated forms of property representation, from "pork belly futures" and real estate investment trusts to junk bonds and derivatives. According to deSoto, capitalist innovators like Michael Milken "were able to reveal and extract capital where others saw only junk by devising new ways to represent the invisible potential that is locked up in assets we accumulate."

These changes did not take place quickly or casually; regions and states adopted formal systems at different intervals. But like the integration of currencies, a uniform system of property and ownership recognition emerged over the life of our nation. As DeSoto puts it,

Over decades in the nineteenth century, politicians, legislators, and judges pulled together the scattered facts and rules that had governed property throughout cities, villages, buildings, and farms and integrated them into one system. This "pulling together" of property representations, a revolutionary moment in the history of developed nations, deposited all the information and rules governing the accumulated wealth of their citizens into one knowledge base.[9]

Making sense of real estate is the first step in this process. Real estate counts for some 50 percent of national wealth in formalized countries; in the southern hemisphere it is closer to 75 percent. In the United States, the first capital that an estimated 70 percent of businesses obtain is secured by loans on real estate. Millions of entrepreneurs secure their enterprises with loans on buildings or their personal homes.

In addition to well-developed property rights, there are other aspects to this socially created system of wealth building. Patents protect the founders of innovations and ideas. Enforceable contracts allow for business deals and long-term projects to be consummated with trust. A system of open courts enforces agreements and rules. Limited liability systems and insurance policies encourage and allow early risks to be taken.

The stock market is a human-created societal asset, with rules and systems that provide a credible and secure way to transact business. This market provides liquidity, which greatly enhances the privately held assets of many businesses. Peter Barnes, founder of a money market fund and long-distance telephone company, recounted his decision to take a company public:

> We retained an investment banker to appraise what the company was worth. What we, the private shareholders, learned was that our business was worth a whole lot more as a public company than as a private company. What added this extra value? It wasn't that we'd make more sales or profit as a public company—these numbers would be the same either way. The extra value came from the fact that our stock would be liquid—we could sell it to any Tom, Dick, or Harriet, any day of the week. According to our investment banker, liquidity alone would add 30 percent to the value of our stock.[10]

For Barnes, this was a pivotal lesson in his business experience. "That added value comes not from the company itself, but from society—from the stock market and the infrastructure of government, financial institutions, and media that supports it." For many whose wealth has been created in the stock market, it is easy to forget that this entire system is a form of socially created wealth. And it is not just any marketplace, where one can rent a stall and hawk goods. It is a highly sophisticated global marketplace, where you can sell your goods virtually anywhere.

A RELIGIOUS PERSPECTIVE ON WEALTH AND SOCIETY
The perspective that society has a claim on individual wealth is reinforced in the teachings of all world religions that we know of. Judaism, Christianity, and Islam all affirm the right of individual ownership and private property, but there are moral limits imposed on absolute private ownership of wealth and property. Each tradition affirms that we are not individuals alone but that we exist in community, a community that makes claims upon us. The notion that "it is all mine" is a violation of these teachings and traditions.[11]

In the Jewish tradition of *tzedakah,* owners of property are required to care for those in need. This is not a matter of charity or choice; it is an obligation. Individual wealth is provided by God, and it is not meant only for "the needs and wants of the private owner, [but] is also meant to be used to satisfy the needs of the poor. . . . So society acquires a property right in the wealth of the individual to provide, through compulsory acts of taxation, the social and charitable needs of its members."[12]

This obligation is rooted in the Hebrew people's experience of being strangers and slaves in the land of Egypt. The memory that the Hebrew people would still be oppressed and still be in Egypt, but for the Grace of God, is the moral basis to welcome and provide for the stranger.

Within the Jewish tradition, individual ownership of wealth —embodied in the notion "This is *all* mine"—is inconsistent with Jewish law, and in the Mishnah may be the mark of the "people of Sodom."[13] Meir Tamari observes, "The Sodomite view of absolute private property rejects any obligations to assist others, which is contrary to the Jewish concept of limited private-property rights."[14]

In the Islamic tradition, the Muslim approach to charity includes both *zakat,* a compulsory component, and *sadaquh,* voluntary giving. *Zakat* is rooted in the individual's obligation as a member of a community. As the prophet Muhammad said, "Like the organs of the body, if one suffers then all others rally in response." *Zakat* "represents the unbreakable bond between members of the community."[15] Since all wealth is owned by God and held by humans in trust, owners of property are not allowed to consider their interests alone.

This notion is similar to the principle of stewardship in the Christian tradition. Riches are granted as a gift from God, and humans are expected to be responsible stewards of this wealth, including sharing it with those less fortunate. Peter J. Gomes notes that "upon those who have wealth, there is a burden of responsibility to use it wisely and not only for themselves." The wealthy must be "generous in proportion to their wealth," because "to whom much is given much is expected."[16]

Catholic bishops have reiterated the notion that there is a "social mortgage on capital," another way to express society's claim. The bishops affirm the importance of private property and ownership and opposition to statist or collectivist approaches. Yet they try to balance our fundamental American aspirations of freedom with society's claim's upon us.

> Support of private ownership does not mean that anyone has the right to unlimited accumulation of wealth. Private property does not constitute for anyone an absolute or unconditioned right. No one is justified in keeping for his exclusive use what he does not need, when others lack necessities.[17]

Part of society's claim is the recognition that owners did not create wealth alone. "They have benefited from the work of many others and from the local communities that support their endeavors."[18] In his encyclical *On Human Work,* Pope John Paul II states that capital "is the result of work and bears the signs of human labor."[19] In other words, those who have labored hold a claim to accumulated wealth and capital.

This notion that society has a claim on individual accumulated wealth has deep roots in world religion. But it is also a fundamentally American notion, rooted in a recognition of society's direct and indirect investment in an individual's success. We didn't get here on our own.

WHAT IS IT WORTH TO BE AN AMERICAN?

One of the encouraging and inspiring dimensions of our effort to preserve the estate tax is that we have heard a number of individuals recounting their life's success not solely as paeans to the "sweat of their brow" but to society's legitimate contribution to their treasure.

Many people pay part of this debt through gifts to charities. They acknowledge their moral obligation to "give back" with contributions to the institutions that helped them get where they are. Many people give to their schools because they recognize the contribution those schools made to them. But there is a duty that goes beyond charities that have directly touched one's life. That duty is to support our government and the role it plays in building and protecting the framework for individual wealth.

Warren Buffet's sentiments about society's investment translate directly into a different attitude toward taxation. In 1993, Berkshire Hathaway paid $390 million in taxes.

> Charlie [Munger] and I have absolutely no complaints about these taxes. We work in a market-based economy that rewards our efforts far more bountifully than it does the efforts of others whose output is of equal or greater benefit to society. Taxation should, and does, partially redress this inequality. But we remain extraordinarily well treated.[20]

Warren Buffett feels that progressive taxation takes into account that some people's skills, like his, are highly valued in the market place. Whereas the skills of other people are undervalued. This is not a function of innate worth but reveals the idiosyncrasies of the market valuing certain skills and gifts. As Warren Buffett explained in a public television interview,

> If you're a marvelous teacher, this world won't pay a lot for it. If you are a terrific nurse, this world will not pay a lot for it. Now, am I going to try to come up with some comparable worth system that some-how redistributes that? No, I don't think you can do that. But I do think that when you're treated enormously well by this market sys-tem, where in effect the market system showers the ability to buy goods and services on you because of some peculiar talent—maybe your adenoids are a certain way, so you can sing and everybody will pay you enormous sums to be on television or whatever—I think so-ciety has a big claim on that.[21]

Individual effort is indispensable to wealth building. But suc-cess is not entirely the result of individual brains and effort. Suc-cess is a product of having been born in this country, a place where education and research are subsidized, where there is an orderly market, where the private sector reaps enormous benefits from public investment. For someone to assert that he or she has grown wealthy in America without the benefit of substantial public in-vestment is pure hubris.

Imagine that God is sitting in his office. He summons before him the next two beings about to be born on earth. He explains to these two spirits that one of them will be born in the United States of America and the other is going to be born in a poor nation in the southern hemisphere. He explains that God's treasury was overinvested in technology stocks and has suffered some losses in recent years and that the heavenly treasury is in need of replen-ishing. God explains that his scheme for raising revenue is to auc-tion off the privilege of birth in the United States.

God is not a nationalist, nor a racist, of course. We don't know if he is a she. But he recognizes that the United States has a won-derful infrastructure of public health, education, and market mechanisms that enhance opportunity. The bargain is that each spirit can write on a piece of paper the percentage of their net worth they are willing to pledge to God's treasury on the day many years later when they die.

Whoever writes a higher number will be born in the United States. Which of these spirits would be so stupid as to write a number as low as 55 percent? What is it worth to operate within this marvelous system? What's wrong with people who accumulate $20 million or $100 million or $500 million putting a third of that back into the place that made possible the enormous accumulation of wealth for them? What is it worth to be an American?

THE ESTATE TAX AND CHARITABLE GIVING

> Without the incentives provided by the estate tax, we're likely to see a decline in the formation of foundations, which are often likely to fund innovative projects that governments and individual donors are less likely to support.
>
> —Edward Cohen[22]

One of the things that makes America great is the vitality of our civic institutions and our nonprofit sector. What if there were no institutions such as universities, youth clubs, religious congregations, hospice programs, children's art programs, human services, amateur sports associations, senior clubs, hospitals, artist colonies, land conservancies, nonprofit housing organizations, fraternal organizations? This list mentions only a very few, but you get the point. Our lives and our communities would be greatly impoverished without these organizations.

Civic and charitable institutions are the protectors of the common good. They occupy the space between the commercial sector and government, commerce and the state, serving as the glue that holds our communities together.

Alexis de Tocqueville saw our civic sector as essential to maintaining a democratic republic in the United States. Our civic institutions "moderate the despotism of the majority and give the people both a taste for freedom and the skills to be free."[23]

> Americans of all ages, all stations in life, and all types of disposition are forever forming associations. There are not only commercial and

industrial associations in which all take part, but others of a thousand different types—religious, moral, serious, futile, very general and very limited, immensely large and very minute. Americans combine to give fetes, found seminaries, build churches, distribute books, and send missionaries to the antipodes. Hospitals, prisons, and schools take shape in that way. Finally, if they want to proclaim a truth or propagate some feeling by the encouragement of a great example, they form an association. In every case, at the head of any new undertaking, where in France you would find the government or in England some territorial magnate, in the United States you are sure to find an association.[24]

De Toqueville remarked that in "the most democratic country in the world" Americans had taken the practice of forming associations "to the highest perfection" of the art. And he poses a question as critical today as it was in 1832: is the strength of American democracy "just an accident, or is there really some necessary connection between associations and equality?"[25]

Go to any small town in America and you will find a boys and girls club, a community-service agency, and a booster club raising money for uniforms for the high school football team. These institutions exist only to the extent people can infuse them with the gifts of their time and money.

In recent years, national observers like Robert Putnam have warned about the erosion of our "social capital," the participatory organizations that anchor our civic health. Putnam warns that as people withdraw into experiencing the world through television or lack the time or will to participate in these civic institutions, our communities become impoverished.[26]

John DiIulio Jr., who was appointed to be President Bush's first director of the Office of Faith-Based and Community Initiatives, knows firsthand the value of such institutions in low-income communities.

> Try imagining this country without organizations like Big Brothers, Big Sisters of America, American Red Cross, America's Promise, Best Friends, Boys and Girls Clubs. The honor roll goes on and on. These organizations number in the hundreds, thousands, and each

day they touch literally millions of lives. Metaphorically speaking, these community-based organizations, religious and secular, are sort of like the army of ants of civil society, leverage each day many times their weight in human and financial good. Or, as I've elsewhere described them, in urban America, they function like the paramedics of civil society, saving lives and restoring health, answering emergencies with daily miracles.[27]

The difference in "social capital" between communities is a contributing factor in public health. As we discussed in chapter 1, communities that lack social capital and strong civic organizations have worse public health conditions, such as a higher incidence of infant mortality or heart disease. Without strong mediating institutions to foster solidarity and a recognition that we are all in the same boat, public health deteriorates. As economic inequality grows in America, one of the hopes for maintaining community—and a sense of the common good—is through our civic institutions.

Our civic sector reflects a partnership between commercial, governmental, and nonprofit organizations. A great deal of the work of government is done through the civic sector.

Where would public education be today without the PTAs and other voluntary associations organized to support the work of teachers, principals, and school boards? These are the folks who pass school levies and who carry the case for our public schools to state legislatures and city councils. Where would our colleges and universities be without their loving and generous alumni associations?

A great deal of innovation and experimentation happens in the civic and nonprofit sector that informs effective government policy. One cannot but wonder where American medicine would be today if the Rockefeller Foundation had not perceived the abysmal state of medical research and education in this country almost a century ago. That foundation financed the transformation of medical research that is the foundation for our advanced medical services today.[28]

At the same time, the civic sector is not a replacement for government. Although we have a much more vibrant independent sector than many similarly developed countries, we also have much higher levels of poverty, infant mortality, and crime. A strong civic sector is not a substitute for a public commitment to a social safety net, which is largely dependent on government support and nonprofit organizations.

The civic sector exists and thrives thanks to contributions of time, treasure, and talents. The funds to sustain the independent sector come from individuals, businesses, and foundations. It is in the establishment and expansion of foundations that the role of charitable bequests and the estate tax needs further exploration.

WILL CHARITIES LOSE WITHOUT THE ESTATE TAX?
During the 2001 debate over the estate tax, there was a limited dialogue over the question of what impact repeal would have on charitable giving. We argued that it would have an adverse effect on this dynamic civic sector.

This is not because we think that people are motivated to give simply because of the tax code. Just as people give millions of volunteer hours a year without tax benefits, many people give their money away without calculating its economic value.

Although we can't know all the diverse motivations people have for giving, the estate tax is certainly an inducement for high-net-worth families to extend their generosity. In the words of Jim Grote, a seasoned fund-raiser, "My experience suggests that while donors give for a variety of reasons (and their generosity is often incredible), few of them ignore the after tax cost of their gifts. I know I don't."[29]

In July 2000, just after Congress passed a repeal of the estate tax for the first time, George Soros described in the *Wall Street Journal* the role of the estate tax in his own significant giving:

> I would be dishonest if I claimed that this consideration [the estate tax deduction] had nothing to do with my decision [to donate to charity]. . . . Abolishing the estate tax would remove one of the main incentives for charitable giving. College presidents and directors of

cultural and charitable organizations ought to be out in force lobbying against it. It is no exaggeration to say that the Death Tax Elimination Act of 2000 would seriously fray our social fabric."[30]

The estate tax does not force a person to be charitable. If someone is not inclined to support charity, he or she would unlikely be
moved by the economic motivation that an heir will get only fifty
or sixty cents of a bequest, but a charity could have a dollar.

The evidence shows, however, that the estate tax makes an
already charitably oriented person deliberately give more. We
know, for instance, that among very-high-net-worth families,
those with estates over $20 million, the estate tax is a significant
incentive to create a charitable foundation or give to an existing
institution, such as a university. Again, this is not entirely because
of the estate tax. Many people give generously over their lifetimes
and set up foundations long before they die. But one motivation is
that, down the road, at the moment when we meet our maker,
there is an estate tax.

Over the last five years, there have been some competing sentiments on this issue. Some proponents of repeal argue that the
impact on charitable giving would be negligible. And one philanthropy expert argues that repealing the estate tax would actually
increase charitable giving and contribute to a "new spirit of
giving."

In the last few years, Americans have given record amounts to
charity.[31] Charitable bequests, given at death, are a significant part
of the picture. Unfortunately, some of the data about charitable
giving and the estate tax is muddled and dated. The Internal Revenue Service hasn't updated some data since the mid-1990s.

In 1995, a total of $8.7 billion in charitable deductions was
made by estates with a total net worth of $111.6 billion. In 1997,
estates provided $14.3 billion to charities. In all years, the amount
from larger estates is quite substantial. In 1997, estates valued below $2.5 million gave $2.6 billion to charity, or 18 percent of the
total allocation. Estates of $5 million or more gave $10.3 billion to
charity, or 72 percent of what all estates gave. The largest share

came from estates valued at $20 million or more, which contributed over $8.3 billion, or 58 percent.

The largest deduction chosen by estates is the unlimited amount that can be given to a surviving spouse. After the marital deduction, the largest deduction for the estate tax is for charitable contributions. Typically more estate dollars are passed on through the spousal deduction than to charity. But for the largest taxable estates of $20 million or more, the amount given to charity in 1997 nearly equaled the amount given to the surviving spouse ($7.47 billion versus $7.53 billion).

As a rule, estates that have tax liability give two to three times as much to charity as estates without tax liability. In 1997, IRS data showed that taxable estates gave to charities 2.1 times the amount that nontaxable estates did.

Where do these bequests go? Historical IRS data about the allocation of charitable bequests give us some indication of which charities might be adversely affected by repeal.[32] Based on data for 1995, we know that the largest number of charitable bequests, over 58 percent, go to religious institutions, accounting for 10 percent of the dollar amount of gifts. An enormous percentage of gifts from smaller estates, those under $5 million, are also largely allocated to churches, synagogues, mosques, and other religious organizations.

Over 60 percent of the dollar amount of bequests goes to scientific, medical, and educational institutions or private foundations. This leads to speculation that without the estate tax, foundations would see a significant reduction in bequests and in their capacity to give. Roughly a third of foundation assets comes from estate bequests, mostly from the largest estates. And coincidentally, 30 percent of the dollar value of bequests goes toward the establishment or expansion of private foundations.

David Joulfaian, who has done some of the most significant research on charitable giving and estate taxes, argues that foundations will take a big hit. "Much of the bequests of the very rich are channeled to benefit such foundations," finds Joulfaian, who sug-

gests that many individuals view foundation bequests as an exten-
sion of their legacy.[33]

Over 31 percent of bequests goes to "education, medical and
science," such as universities, hospitals, and scientific research in-
stitutes. About 3 percent goes to arts and humanities. Only 1 percent of bequests is directed to social welfare groups promoting
civil rights, community development, social science research, or
government effectiveness. But these organizations rely heavily on
private foundations, so they would be adversely affected by a reduction in bequests to foundations as well.[34]

Bequests from estates don't just benefit the large-scale charities, such as universities and hospitals that have planned giving
programs. Because a third of bequests go to existing or new foundations, this money is regranted through numerous programs that
reach very local and small-scale charities. As a result, the local boys
and girls club or antihunger agency benefits from the inducement
of the estate tax.

Some individuals who work with very wealthy families don't
view the elimination of the estate tax as having a significant impact on giving. In the experience of Arnold Mullen, a business and
financial planner in West Palm Beach, many wealthy people generally don't want to leave vast sums of money to their children for
fear they will become slothful and dissolute. "They want their
children to be productive, including performing charitable activities," said Mullen. "What they don't want is them sitting on the
beach all day drinking martinis."[35]

Stuart Butler of the Heritage Foundation argues that estimates
of declining estate gifts do not consider whether wealthy people
might give an offsetting amount to charity while alive if there
were no estate tax. "People tend to think in their working lives
that they want to give to charity," reasons Butler. "If the estate tax
makes it attractive to do it in an estate, then that's how they'll do
it." But the estate tax provides no penalty for giving while alive;
rather the opposite: there is an inducement as gifts while living reduce the size of the estate.[36]

A NEW SPIRIT OF GIVING?

Paul Schervish, a professor and researcher at Boston College, wrote one of the most widely quoted articles on the impact of estate taxation on charity.[37] He argued that philanthropy would not only survive but thrive without the tax. Schervish, who once supported the estate tax, now believes that repealing the tax would "lead to greater national and personal economic growth, encourage charitable giving to be more of a voluntary act than one spurred by tax incentives, and mobilize for charity the increasing affluence and philanthropic inclinations of many Americans."

Schervish argues that charities would be better off not lobbying for the tax, but rather should plan "how to become effective in an environment in which contributions can flow to them through a far less circuitous and expensive route than what the estate tax creates."

Schervish's arguments are based on data collected over the last decade showing that charitable bequests are growing and that wealthy people are already shifting their legacies to charity prior to death. Schervish also cites his extensive interviews with 112 wealthy people with assets of $5 million or more about "their expected and desired allocations of their estates to heirs, taxes and charity."

What Schervish found was that under current laws, these wealthy individuals expect that 16 percent of their estates will go to charity, 47 percent to heirs, and 37 percent to taxes. When asked what their desires were, they stated that they would like 26 percent to go to charity, 64 percent to go to heirs, and only 9 percent to go to taxes. Schervish draws the conclusion, based on these stated preferences, that without the lash of estate taxes, there would be a 63 percent *increase* in charitable bequests.

Schervish is a believer in the possibilities inherent in a "new spirit of giving." Doing away with the estate tax would "increase not only the amount of giving, but also the quality of giving."

> Indeed, [repeal of the estate tax] would be the basis for a new
> era of spiritual depth in philanthropy, making the voluntary act

of charity more fully a work of liberty and humanitarian care, and less the windfall fruit of a convoluted tax strategy. . . . The benefits of repeal, in the form of increased giving that is spurred by greater affluence and spirituality inspired beneficence, rather than tax policy, are ones that all of philanthropy should embrace.

While we are familiar with the experience and inspiration of the "new spirit of giving," we also find some of Schervish's findings alarming. Even the sentiments in his limited sample, we believe, strengthen the case for the estate tax.

Although his interviews reveal a stated intention by wealthy individuals to increase their donations to charity by 63 percent— they also state they would like to decrease their taxes by 76 percent and increase the inheritances of their heirs by 40 percent. The combined 18 percent decline in resources going to the civic and public sphere makes a pretty good case for not encouraging the super-wealthy to dictate tax policy!

Indeed, the preponderance of other research studies show that estate tax repeal will reduce contributions to charity, both over the donor's lifetime and at death. A study commissioned by the Independent Sector and the Council on Foundations estimates that elimination of the estate tax in 1996 would have reduced charitable bequests by $3 billion in that year.[38] Extrapolating from these 1996 estimates, there would have been a decline of $7.3 billion in 2001.[39]

During his tenure as secretary of the U.S. treasury, Harvard University president Lawrence Summers commissioned a study on the impact of repeal that showed that contributions to charity would decline by an annual loss of $5 billion to $6 billion in 1999.[40]

The most recent research, conducted by David Joulfaian, found that the deductibility of bequests has a significant effect on giving. Using a conservative set of variables, he estimates that "charitable giving may decline by some 13 percent in the absence of the estate tax." Using other variables, he suggests it might decline by as much as 31 percent. Overall, he argues, "the higher the tax rate the greater the giving" and the higher the estate tax, the costlier it is to make transfers to heirs.[41]

We anticipate that the growth of wealth in the last two decades will mean that the estate tax could have an even more significant effect in the future. After all, estimates of the intergenerational transfer of wealth in the next twenty years run as high as $50 trillion. An estate tax could generate very significant revenue and be a considerable incentive to charitable giving.[42]

WHAT ABOUT THE CHILDREN?
THE DANGERS OF THE SILVER SPOON
If we were as imaginative as the proponents of repeal, we would undertake a national advertising campaign featuring hundreds of well-known child psychologists. Imagine a full-page newspaper advertisement stating, "The undersigned three hundred prominent child psychologists support preservation of the estate tax because of the adverse and psychologically damaging effects of significant inherited wealth on children."

This is a secondary argument for preserving the estate tax. Some might regard a discussion of the imprudence of passing on substantial inherited wealth to children as improper in a policy discussion. We include it, not only because it is part of the historic debate, but because it may be an example of where the public interest and the long-term interest of heirs might both be best served by the estate tax and a limit on hereditary wealth transfers.

When we talk about inheritance, we are not referring to the experience of people who inherit a small-scale family enterprise, such as a farm or the corner pharmacy, and continue the work that their parents did. These are legacies linked to ongoing work, not passive ownership. We are referring to those who inherit such substantial capital that they actually don't have to earn a living in the marketplace.

It is widely recognized, both in contemporary psychology and in the biographical histories of those with tremendous inherited wealth, that giving an heir so much money that he or she never has to work is a barbed gift.

After the technology boom of the 1990s, there was a proliferation of wealth counseling services for the children of parents experiencing "sudden wealth syndrome." Modern day wealth counselors advise wealthy parents on how to enable their children to grow up with healthy attitudes about money and stewardship and without separating themselves from the mass of humanity.

There is widespread affirmation of Andrew Carnegie's observation that "the parent who leaves his son enormous wealth generally deadens the talents and energies of [his child], and leads him to lead a less useful and less worthy life than he otherwise would." Andrew Carnegie regarded leaving wealth to descendants as "most injudicious." In *The Gospel of Wealth,* Carnegie wrote about how destructive the land tenure system in monarchical societies had been that left all property to the oldest son. And then his famous quote:

> Why should men leave great fortunes to their children? If this is done from affection, is it not misguided affection? Observation teaches that, generally speaking, it is not well for the children that they should be so burdened. Neither is it well for the State. . . . For it is no longer questionable that great sums bequeathed often work more for the injury than for the good of the recipients. Wise men will soon conclude that, for the best interests of the members of their families, and of the State, such bequests are an improper use of their means.[43]

Carnegie made an exception for progeny who are laboring for "public ends without reference to pecuniary considerations." In other words, heirs who devote their lives to community service of some kind while living off of wealth might be worthy of endowment. Carnegie argued that this was a rare exception, and after looking over the results of inherited wealth, a thoughtful person would not leave a substantial inheritance. "I would as soon leave to my son a curse as the almighty dollar," said Carnegie. The donor should admit to themselves that it is "not the welfare of the children, but family pride, which inspires these legacies."[44]

Carnegie believed that wealthy individuals should give away all their wealth during their lifetime, not leave it for heirs. Even leaving wealth at death for public purposes, thought Carnegie, means the donor "is content to wait until he is dead before he becomes of much good in the world."

Carnegie believed, however, that a lot of legacies were not well used and that the wishes of the donors were often thwarted. "Men who leave vast sums in this way may fairly be thought men who would not have left it at all had they been able to take it with them." This arouses speculation that they were holding out for eternal life and the proverbial hearse with the U-Haul trailer. "The memories of such cannot be held in grateful remembrance, for there is no grace in their gifts. It is not to be wondered at that such bequests seem so generally to lack the blessing."[45]

In *The Millionaire Next Door,* a contemporary examination of wealth, Thomas J. Stanley and William D. Danko point out that "lifetime and testamentary family gifts are both a disincentive to work as well as a disincentive to save." Their findings show that the more dollars adult children receive, the fewer they accumulate, while those who are given fewer dollars accumulate more. This is because some wealthy families provide their children with what Stanley and Danko call "economic outpatient care." This care takes the form of subsidies for education, housing, and ongoing cash infusions. Based on Stanley and Danko's extensive interviews, recipients of "outpatient care" tend to rely on their parents' wealth and live in anticipation of future inheritances. As a result, recipients spend beyond their earnings, take on substantial debt, remain unemployed or underemployed, fail to save money, and lack entrepreneurial motivation.

In their research, Stanley and Danko find that "economic outpatient care" is the single most significant factor that explains the lack of productivity among the adult children of the affluent.[46] They were amazed by their interviews with recipients of parental subsidies. They report that "two of every three adults who receive significant cash gifts periodically from their parents view themselves as members of the 'I did it on my own' club. We are amazed when these people tell us in interviews, 'We earned every dollar we have.' "[47]

These "self-made" inheritors live out the mythology we discussed earlier in this chapter, the notion that "they didn't get any help" in their good fortune. But Stanley and Danko report that these individuals live with greater anxieties than those who have built wealth on their own. For recipients of "economic outpatient care, their biggest anxiety is that their parents' estate will be heavily taxed."[48] Since they are ill prepared to earn their own way in the world, they are understandably fearful of losing even part of their inheritance.

Inherited wealth can sometimes create generations of dependency that are as debilitating as the stereotype about low-income welfare dependency. As Warren Buffet pointed out, "The Duponts might believe themselves perceptive in observing the debilitating effects of food stamps for the poor, but were themselves living off a boundless supply of privately funded food stamps. . . . The idea that you get a lifetime of food stamps based on coming out of the right womb strikes at my idea of fairness."[49]

A large portion of wealth in the United States is dynastic, passing from wealthy parents to children. An estimated 50 percent of wealth in the United States is inherited. Some have argued that the harmful effects of wealth on the media and democracy are stronger in the case of dynastic wealth compared with wealth held by different families in each generation. With dynastic wealth, James Repetti notes, it "is less certain that the subsequent generations will have new perspectives, life experiences, or great talent."[50] John Maynard Keynes was a bit more blunt: "The hereditary principle in the transmission of wealth and the control of business is the reason why the leadership of the capitalist cause is weak and stupid."[51]

The more a society is organized around the preservation of wealth for those who already have it, rather than building new wealth, the more impoverished we will all be.

The Estate Tax and the Common Good

What is most important for democracy is not that great fortunes
should not exist, but that great fortunes should not remain in the
same hands.

—Alexis de Tocqueville

For many ordinary Americans, the estate tax is a remote issue in
their lives. The vast majority will never pay it, nor do they per-
ceive any particular benefit from it. Its revenue flows into the
treasury, paying for general government services, the benefits of
which are often difficult to see during the course of daily life.

Although we are uncomfortable in principle with "earmarked" or dedicated revenue sources, we are intrigued by the
possibilities of linking estate tax revenue to government programs
such as enhancing the Social Security trust fund or providing
medical care to the unemployed and elderly.

It is our view that public support for the estate tax would
greatly increase if people saw a direct connection between the tax
and their quality of life. There is something poetic about allocating estate tax revenues to particular initiatives that strengthen
equality of opportunity in America.

In the years after World War II, a large percentage of Americans benefited from the G.I. Bill, particularly in the form of a
debt-free college education. Still more received very-low-interest
mortgages to purchase their first home, getting a government-
backed boost onto the wealth-building train. We would be hard-

pressed to find a member of the postwar generation who questioned the prudence of this investment.

For this reason, we advocate that the estate tax be preserved and that its revenue be directly linked to supplementing Social Security or directed to an educational trust fund to provide a modern-day GI Bill for education. This would make more evident the moral rationale of how the tax is part of the investment society makes in individuals. When people are extremely enriched, society recaptures that part of its investment and ensures that it is available to subsequent generations.

Revenue from the estate tax could capitalize a federally administered educational trust fund that provides grants and zero-interest loans for college education. Such a fund could have the impact that the GI Bill had for an earlier generation. Too many young people are unable to afford the cost of going to college and graduate with a double whammy of enormous school loans and personal consumer debt.

Researchers have shown that over the next seventy-five years the Social Security deficit approaches the amount of revenue that would be lost if the federal estate tax were repealed. Dedicating estate tax revenue to the Social Security trust fund addresses a long-term fiscal problem—how to maintain our commitment to retirees without cutting benefits or imposing an even greater payroll tax burden on the next generation of workers.

The point is that revenue from the estate tax should go directly to initiatives that maintain retirement security or assist in building wealth and opportunity for everyone. As a society, we do a great many things to create opportunity. When the fortunate few accumulate vast wealth as a result of their effort and society's investment, then we should celebrate this achievement and recapture a part of our investment. This investment should be recycled for subsequent generations, possibly in the form of a debt-free college education or retirement security for all workers.

Of course, there is always room to talk about improving the specifics of the estate tax. Throughout the debate over the estate tax our position has been "mend it, don't end it." We advocate for reform: increasing the exemptions, changing the rates, and simplifying the tax. These changes would make the estate tax fairer, generate substantial revenue, and reduce compliance costs.

Many of the concerns people raise about the estate tax could be addressed by increasing the amount of wealth exempted from the tax. The 2001 tax-cut legislation raises the estate tax exemption for a single individual to $3.5 million in 2009, before the tax is eliminated the following year ($7 million for a couple). This is a fair exemption and further targets the tax on those most able to pay. With such high exemptions, many people will not even have to consider planning.

If exemptions were raised to $3.5 million, we know that fewer than six thousand estates would have paid an estate tax in 1999. In thirty-three states there were fewer than one hundred taxable estates that were valued at $3.5 million or more. States such as Arkansas, Idaho, Maine, Mississippi, Montana, New Hampshire, New Mexico, North Dakota, South Dakota, Wyoming, Vermont, and Utah would each have had fewer than twenty-five estates valued over $3.5 million; Alaska would have had six. The states that would have had the highest number of estates valued over $3.5 million would be New York (422), Florida (574), and California (880).[1]

Estate tax reform proposals with such high exemptions have been blocked by all-or-nothing repeal forces. But one has to wonder about congressional representatives in states like Montana, Arkansas, or Arizona, who expend so much political capital to protect a handful of wealthy citizens in exchange for not having the resources to meet the needs of other constituencies.

The 2001 tax law reduces the top rate of the tax. Although econometric research on this rate cut is still outstanding, it will likely reduce the progressivity of the tax. We would advocate reducing the rates at the bottom end but retaining the high top tax rate of 55 percent. This would keep the effective rate at somewhere between 25 and 35 percent, a reasonable toll on the recipients of very substantial wealth.

We might also consider a more graduated rate structure. Recall that during World War II the estate tax rate was 70 percent on wealth over $50 million. At present, the top rate is imposed on wealth over $3 million. But there is no reason why the bottom rate could not be lower—and there be higher rate structures for wealth thresholds above $20 million and $50 million.

Reform proposals of the future will no doubt center around the issue of what constitutes a "qualified family-owned business." Such a designation makes sense, but not if it becomes a stealth loophole that enables any enterprise to qualify, no matter how large. Beware of exemptions that are so large that some of large family corporations mentioned earlier might attempt to qualify.

Estate tax reform should better target the tax to those with the greatest ability to pay and reduce the number of estates that would have to plan for and comply with the tax. With a more graduated rate structure at the top, the estate tax could capture more wealth from the super-wealthy—and be more effective at interrupting the buildup of accumulated wealth.

In the same way that Paul Schervish talks about a new spirit of giving, we propose *a new spirit of paying taxes,* particularly among the wealthiest few. This new spirit wouldn't hold a grudging resentment toward the public sector nor would it view the tax collector as an alien invader and the tax burden as an obligation to be circumvented.

This spirit of paying taxes exists in the United States, even in these feverishly antitax times. At a conference in 2001, we were approached by a man in his seventies who quietly told us that his father had died the previous year and he had just written an estate tax check to the government for five hundred thousand dollars. He said he felt good about it and that his father would have been proud. He didn't want to be boastful, so he hadn't told anyone about it.

A new "spirit of taxation" would invoke Supreme Court justice Oliver Wendell Holmes's dictum that "taxes are the price we pay for civilization." Taxes are a privilege in a democratic society, a necessary component for sustaining the common good. And progressive taxes are a fair tribute to a society that has created the conditions that enable some individuals to become wealthy and prosperous.

Anyone interested in the national movement to reform the estate tax, but not repeal it, can learn more at www.responsible wealth.org. We send out periodic action alerts and updates and welcome involvement. You can write to us at: Responsible Wealth, 37 Temple Place, 2nd Floor, Boston, MA 02111. Or email us at authors@responsiblewealth.org.

NOTES

Introduction

1. We are still enlisting individuals to sign this petition at *www.responsible-wealth.org*.

2. Sheldon Cohen, former IRS commissioner, from Jeffrey H. Birnbaum and Alan S. Murray, *Showdown at Gucci Gulch: Lawyers, Lobbyists, and the Unlikely Triumph of Tax Reform* (New York: Random House, 1987), p. 289.

3. While there were sufficient votes in the Senate (including that of Senator Jeffords) to pass the law, procedurally the Senate leadership would have slowed down the pace, perhaps long enough for new surplus projections to emerge. In any event, a conference committee process to reconcile the bill would have also slowed down or stopped final passage of the bill.

4. William G. Gale and Samara R. Potter, "An Economic Evaluation of the Economic Growth and Tax Relief Reconciliation Act of 2001," *National Tax Journal,* March 2002.

5. Under the 1997 Tax Reform Act, the estate tax exemptions are already scheduled to rise to $1 million by 2006, so the law will revert back to the scheduled changes.

6. Paul Krugman, "Bad Heir Day," *New York Times,* May 29, 2001.

7. Estimate from the Joint Tax Committee, as cited in Gale and Potter, "Economic Evaluation."

8. Greenberg Quinlan Rosner Research, "Attitudes about the Estate Tax," poll conducted May 6–9, 2002, one thousand respondents.

1. What Kind of Nation Do We Want to Be?

1. Will Hutton, "Log Cabin to White House? Not Any More," *Observer of London,* April 28, 2002.

2. Gale and Potter, "Economic Evaluation," p. 17.

3. John J. Havens and Paul Schervish, "Millionaires and the Millennium: New Estimates of the Forthcoming Wealth Transfer and the Prospects for a Golden

Age of Philanthropy," Boston College Social Welfare Research Institute, October 19, 1999.

4. Paul Schervish, "The New Philanthropists," *Boston Globe,* March 3, 2002.

5. "The Forbes Four Hundred," *Forbes Magazine,* September 13, 1982.

6. Kevin Sack, "States Expecting to Lose Billions from Repeal of the U.S. Estate Tax," *New York Times,* June 21, 2001.

7. John Harwood, "Tighter State Budgets May Mean Closer Governor's Races," *Wall Street Journal,* August 7, 2001.

8. During 2002, a number of states started to unlink their state inheritance and estate taxes from the federal estate tax in order to preserve revenue. See Robert McIntyre, "The Taxonomist," *American Prospect,* June 3, 2002.

9. Sidney Ratner, *Taxation and Democracy in America,* rev. ed. (New York: Wiley, 1967), p. 260.

10. Edward N. Wolff, *Top Heavy: The Increasing Inequality of Wealth in America and What Can Be Done about It* (New York: New Press, 2002). Also see Kevin Phillips, *Wealth and Democracy: A Political History of the American Rich* (New York: Broadway Books, 2002).

11. Lawrence Mishel, Jared Bernstein, and John Schmitt, *The State of Working America, 2000–2001* (Ithaca, N.Y.: ILR Press, 2001), table 2-6, p. 124. Updated to 2000 using Economic Policy Institute Quarterly Wage and Employment Series, fourth quarter 2000, table 3.

12. Data from the World Bank, as prepared by Public Agenda in 1996, as cited in Phillips, *Wealth and Democracy,* pp. 123–25, chart 3–6, "The United States Leads in Inequality."

13. See Robert Pollin and Stephanie Luce, *The Living Wage: Building a Fair Economy* (New York: New Press, 1998).

14. U.S. Census Bureau, *Fertility of American Women,* June Current Population Survey, 1998, pp. 9 and 12. "In 1998, two-earner families became the majority of all married-couple families." From Dulcy Anderson and Charles C. Euchner, "The Dilemmas of Family Leave," *Boston Globe,* April 22, 2002.

15. "Executive Pay," *Business Week,* April 16, 2001.

16. James L. Huston, *Securing the Fruits of Labor: The American Concept of Wealth Distribution, 1765–1900* (Baton Rouge: University of Louisiana Press, 1998), pp. 83–85. These data have great limitations, as statistical calculations of wealth measured different things and were not comprehensive until the early twentieth century.

17. Wolff, *Top Heavy,* p. 9.

18. The top tax rate during this period was 90 percent, though there were many loopholes that reduced the effective rate.

19. Wealth data from Wolff, *Top Heavy*, p. 9. Even though it was a time of relatively greater shared prosperity, we should not overromanticize those two decades. See Stephanie Coontz, *The Way We Never Were: American Families and the Nostalgia Trap* (New York: Basic Books, 2000).

20. Wolff, *Top Heavy*, pp. 8–9. Also see Chuck Collins, Betsy Leondar-Wright, and Holly Sklar, *Shifting Fortunes: The Perils of the Growing American Wealth Gap* (Boston: United for a Fair Economy, 1999).

21. Wolff, *Top Heavy*, pp. 28–29.

22. Bureau of Economic Analysis, "Personal Saving as a Percentage of Disposable Personal Income," National Accounts Data, from *www.bea.doc.gov/bea/dn1.htm,* updated August 2, 2002.

23. Edward Wolff, "Recent Trends in Wealth Ownership, 1983–1998," Levy Economics Institute working paper no. 300, April 2000 (*www.levy.org/docs/wrkpap/papers/300.html*), based on a Federal Reserve Survey of Consumer Finances. Financial wealth is net worth minus net equity in owner-occupied housing. These numbers will be updated in 2002. For more about racial wealth disparities, see Collins, Leondar-Wright, and Sklar, *Shifting Fortunes,* pp. 55–59.

24. This shift in the tax burden has been discussed in a number of recent examinations of inequality. See Donald L. Barlett and James B. Steele, *America: Who Really Pays the Taxes* (New York: Simon & Schuster, 1994); and Donald L. Barlett and James B. Steele, *The Great American Tax Dodge* (Boston: Little, Brown, 2000). Also see Charles Lewis, Bill Allison, and the Center for Public Integrity, *The Cheating of America: How Tax Avoidance and Evasion by the Super Rich Are Costing the Country Billions—and What You Can Do about It* (New York: HarperCollins, 2001).

25. Jeff Gates, *Democracy at Risk: Rescuing Main Street from Wall Street* (Cambridge, Mass.: Perseus Press, 2000), p. xii.

26. Phillips, *Wealth and Democracy,* p. 118.

27. Samuel Huntington as quoted in Phillips, *Wealth and Democracy,* p. xv.

28. John Nichols and Robert W. McChesney, *It's the Media, Stupid* (New York: Seven Stories Press, 2000). The big nine are AOL–Time Warner, Disney, Rupert Murdoch's NewsCorp, Viacom, Sony, Seagram (Universal), AT&T/Liberty Media, Bertelsmann, and General Electric. They have revenues between $6 billion and $30 billion a year, and each controls a wide variety of media holdings that include film, radio, television, and newspapers. Another twelve to fifteen firms, which do between $2 billion and $8 billion a year in business, are less diversified and control only two or three different news mediums.

These include Washington Post, Cox, New York Times, Hearst, Advance, Tribune Company, and Gannett (Nichols and McChensey, *It's the Media,* pp. 16 and 28). This concentration, compared with that of two generations ago, should give us pause. But will we hear about it on television?

29. Center for Responsive Politics, "Election Overview, 2000 Cycle," *www.opensecrets.org.*

30. John Green, Paul Hermson, Lynda Powell, Clyde Wilcox, and the Center for Responsive Politics, "Individual Congressional Campaign Contributors: Wealthy, Conservative and Reform-Minded," *www.opensecrets.org/pubs/donors/donors.asp,* June 9, 1998.

31. For survey of research see James R. Repetti, "Democracy, Taxes and Wealth," *New York University Law Review,* June 2001.

32. Lisa A. Keister, *Wealth in America: Trends in Wealth Inequality* (Cambridge: Cambridge University Press, 2000), pp. 196–98. Updated data for 1998 discussed in Lisa A. Keister, "The Estate Tax as Robin Hood?" *American Prospect,* May 21, 2001.

33. See Kevin Phillips's discussion of financialization, politics, and "capitalist heydays" in *Wealth and Democracy,* pp. 293–316.

34. Sam Pizzigati, "America Needs More Than a Raise," *Working USA,* September/October 1997, p. 76.

35. Philippe Aghion, Eve Caroli, and Cecilia Garcia-Peñalosa, "Inequality and Economic Growth: The Perspective of the New Growth Theories," *Journal of Economic Literature 1615–1617* 37, no. 4 (December 1999). Also Alberto Alesina and Dani Rodrik, "Distribution, Political Conflict, and Economic Growth: A Simple Theory and Some Empirical Evidence," in Alex Cukierman, Zvi Hercowitz, and Leonardo Leiderman, eds., *Political Economy, Growth, and Business Cycles* (Cambridge: MIT Press, 1992), pp. 23–24. For a good survey of these arguments see Repetti, "Democracy, Taxes, and Wealth."

36. See Roberto Perotti, "Growth, Income Distribution, and Democracy: What the Data Say," *Journal of Economic Growth* 1, no. 2 (1996): 149–87. Also see Jess Benhabib and Aldo Rustichini, "Social Conflict and Growth," *Journal of Economic Growth* 1, no. 1 (1996): 125–42.

37. David Kennedy, *Freedom from Fear: The American People in Depression and War, 1929–1945* (New York: Oxford University Press, 1999), p. 21.

38. Jeff Gates, *The Ownership Solution: Toward a Shared Capitalism for the Twenty-first Century* (Reading, Mass.: Addison Wesley, 1998), pp. 207–8.

39. Gates, *Ownership Solution.* Also see Gates, *Democracy at Risk.*

40. Ichiro Kawachi, Bruce Kennedy, and Richard Wilkinson, eds., *Income Inequality and Health: A Reader* (New York: New Press, 1999). Thanks to Ste-

phen Bezruchka at the University of Washington for his assistance with this section. His research, teaching, and writing on this topic are prolific.

41. Richard Wilkinson, *Unhealthy Societies: The Afflictions of Inequality* (London: Routledge, 1996), p. 102.

42. Edward J. Blakely and Mary Gail Snyder, *Fortress America: Gated Communities in the United States* (Washington, D.C.: Brookings Institution Press, 1997). Justice Policy Institute Study, as reported in Jesse Katy, "A Nation of Too Many Prisoners?" *Los Angeles Times,* February 15, 2000.

43. Keister, "Estate Tax as Robin Hood?"

44. Keister, *Wealth in America,* pp. 196–98. Updated data for 1998 discussed in Keister, "Estate Tax as Robin Hood?"

45. Edward Wolff, *Top Heavy,* p. 12.

2. The Origins of America's Estate Tax

1. Alexis de Tocqueville, *Democracy in America* (New York: Harper & Row, 1969), bk. 2, p. 506.

2. Kennedy, *Freedom from Fear,* p. 387.

3. This chapter is greatly indebted to several historians of inequality and taxation, including James L. Huston (*Securing the Fruits of Labor*) and Sidney Ratner (*Taxation and Democracy*).

4. Thomas Paine, *Common Sense* (New York: Barnes & Noble, 1995), p. 14.

5. Jim Grote writes in his unpublished essay "Is Unlimited Inheritance Un-American?" that Paine proposed an inheritance tax that would be used to create a national fund that (1) would give the sum of fifteen pounds sterling to everyone turning twenty-one years old as compensation for the loss of their "natural inheritance," and (2) would give a sum of ten pounds a year to every person over the age of fifty as an early version of Social Security.

6. Huston, *Securing the Fruits of Labor,* p. 25.

7. George Rappoport, *Stability and Change in Revolutionary Pennsylvania* (University Park, Pa.: 1996) p. 119. Thanks to Jim Grote for pointing out this quote. Also cited in Phillips, *Wealth and Democracy,* p. 6.

8. Noah Webster, *An Examination into the Leading Principles of the Federal Constitution, Proposed by the Late Convention Held at Philadelphia* (Philadelphia, 1787), 47.

9. David McCullough, *John Adams* (New York: Simon & Schuster, 2001), p. 102; Huston, *Securing the Fruits of Labor,* pp. 21–22.

10. Huston, *Securing the Fruits of Labor,* p. 21.

11. John Adams to James Sullivan, May 26, 1776, in Charles Francis Adams, ed., *The Works of John Adams, Second President of the United States* (Boston, 1856), 9:376–77.

12. Thomas Jefferson writing to James Madison, dated October 28, 1785, as cited in Peter Barnes, *The People's Land* (Emmaus, Pa.: Rodale Press, 1975), pp. 3–4.

13. Ibid.

14. Huston, *Securing the Fruits of Labor,* p. 22.

15. McCullough describes the mean-spirited campaign of accusations against Adams in *John Adams,* pp. 543–47. McCullough writes that one of the great ironies was that "Jefferson, the Virginia aristocrat and slave master who lived in a style fit for a prince, as removed from his fellow citizens and their lives as it was possible to be, was hailed as the apostle of liberty, the 'Man of the People.' Adams, the farmer's son who despised slavery and practices the kind of personal economy and plain living commonly upheld as the American way, was scorned as an aristocrat who, if he could, would enslave the common people."

16. See Huston, *Securing the Fruits of Labor,* chapter 2, "The Enemy of the Republic: The Political Economy of Aristocracy."

17. Ibid., p. 56.

18. Kevin Phillips notes that the southern colonies were the wealthiest in North America because of slave ownership, which constituted half of the South's wealth at the time of the American Revolution. Phillips, *Wealth and Democracy,* p. 8.

19. Huston, *Securing the Fruits of Labor,* p. 27.

20. Ibid., pp. 44–47.

21. Joseph J. Ellis, "The Big Man: History vs. Alexander Hamilton," *The New Yorker,* October 29, 2001.

22. Huston writes that "the parties tended to divide on . . . Jeffersonian adherents versus Hamiltonian followers. In both instances, however, politicians relentlessly paraded their allegiance to the labor theory of property/value and the fear of aristocratic control of the economy" (*Securing the Fruits of Labor,* p. xvii).

23. Ellis, "Big Man." Also Joseph J. Ellis, *Founding Brothers: The Revolutionary Generation* (New York: Random House, 2000).

24. Huston, *Securing the Fruits of Labor,* p. 344.

25. Henry George, *Progress and Poverty* (New York: Robert Schalkenbach Foundation, 1975). George challenged Theodore Roosevelt in a race to be governor of New York. Although he lost, his devoted "single tax" followers advocated for

breaking up concentrations of land ownership. To this day, followers of Henry George advocate for recognition of society's claim on appreciated value in absentee-owned property.

26. Huston, *Securing the Fruits of Labor,* p. 349.

27. Ibid., p. xviii.

28. Smaller producers were squeezed out or absorbed. By 1877, the Standard Oil Company controlled 85 to 90 percent of oil refining and was actively controlling production and distribution. Chernow, *Titan: The Life of John D. Rockefeller Sr.* (New York: Random House, 1998), pp. 205–6.

29. The political arena was rife with bribery and corruption. Long before any campaign finance or disclosure laws existed, the influence of money on politics was unbridled. The large trusts gave trunkloads of cash directly to candidates with the intention of buying elections. It was widely accepted that the large trusts and their fund-raising master, Mark Hanna, purchased the presidency in 1896 for William McKinley. President McKinley did not disappoint his patrons as he blocked populist reforms aimed at the trusts. For more on the "shame of the Senate," see Matthew Josephson, *The Robber Barons* (San Diego, Calif.: Harcourt, Brace, 1934); and Edmund Morris, *Theodore Rex* (New York: Random House, 2001).

30. Lawrence Goodwyn, *Democratic Promise: The Populist Moment in American* (New York: Oxford University Press, 1976); and Michael Kazin, *Populist Persuasion: An American History* (New York: HarperCollins, 1995).

31. Norman J. Ware, *The Labor Movement in the United States, 1860–1895: A Study in Democracy* (New York: Vintage Books, 1964). Statistics also covered in Chernow, *Titan,* p. 294.

32. Ware, *Labor Movement.* See also Jeremy Brecher, *Strike!* (Boston: South End Press, 1972).

33. Chernow, *Titan,* p. 334.

34. Ratner, *Taxation and Democracy,* p. 258, citing John R. Commons, *History of Labor in the United States* (Kelley, 1966), 3:293ff., 660–700, 4:13ff.; Leo Wolman, *Ebb and Flow in Trade Unionism* (New York, 1936), pp. 15–20.

35. Ida Tarbel wrote a series of exposés of Standard Oil in *McClure's* magazine that were credited with greatly changing public attitudes toward the trusts. Theodore Roosevelt personally read Tarbel's "The Oil War of 1872." See Morris, *Theodore Rex,* pp. 194–95. Lincoln Steffens' series, "Shame of the Cities," chronicled bribery, machine politics, and other corruption of several major American cities. The original Steffens articles were also featured in *McClure's.* Henry Demarest Lloyd wrote *Wealth against Commonwealth* in 1894.

36. Theologian Charles Strong wrote an essay that he read aloud to his father-

in-law, John D. Rockefeller, "on the duties of rich men, arguing that when people accumulated wealth on a colossal scale, they should then convert that wealth into public trusts, administered by trustees for the commonweal." Historian Ron Chernow (*Titan*, p. 530) speculates that this essay might have strengthened Rockefeller's wish to create a huge philanthropic foundation.

37. *Rerum Novarum* was published May 15, 1891. See William J. Gibbons, ed., *Seven Great Encyclicals* (New York: Paulist Press, 1963); and Joseph Moody, *Church and Society: Catholic Social and Political Thought and Movements, 1789–1950* (New York: Arts, 1953).

38. Huston, *Securing the Fruits of Labor*, p. 347. From an article Pomeroy wrote, "The Concentration of Wealth," in *Arena* 58(1896): 89–91, 95.

39. Ratner, *Taxation and Democracy*, p. 235.

40. Ibid.

41. Sources for this section are Ratner, *Taxation and Democracy*, and John F. Witte, *The Politics and Development of the Federal Income Tax* (Madison: University of Wisconsin Press, 1985). For a discussion of wartime taxation and profiteering, see Stuart D. Brandes, *Warhogs: A History of War Profits in America* (Lexington: University Press of Kentucky, 1997).

42. Huston, *Securing the Fruits of Labor*, p. 356, citing Harold C. Livesay, *Andrew Carnegie and the Rise of Big Business* (Boston: Addison-Wesley, 1975), pp. 187–88. Also see Ron Chernow, *The House of Morgan* (New York: Simon & Schuster, 1990), pp. 83–85.

43. Andrew Carnegie, "The Gospel of Wealth," was originally published as "Wealth" in the *North American Review* in 1889. Andrew Carnegie, *The Gospel of Wealth* (Cambridge: Harvard University Press, Belknap Press, 1962), p. 21.

44. Ibid.

45. Ibid., p. 22.

46. Peter Dobkin Hall, ed., *A Documentary History of Philanthropy and Voluntarism in America,* an on-line curricular resource. See http://ksghome.harvard.edu/phall.hauser.ksg/responsiblewealth.html.

47. Ibid., p. 5 of 31.

48. Chernow, *Titan*, p. 567.

49. Ibid., p. 529.

50. Ibid., pp. 566–67.

51. Theodore Roosevelt, *Works* (20 volumes) (New York, 1926), 16:415, 421. As cited in Ratner, *Taxation and Democracy*, p. 260.

52. Paul L. Menchik and Nancy A. Jianakoplos, "Economics of Inheritance," in

Inheritance and Wealth in America, ed. Robert K. Miller Jr. and Stephen J. McNamee (New York and London: Plenum Press, 1998), p. 71.

53. Theodore Roosevelt, *Presidential Addresses* (8 volumes) (New York, 1910), 6:1319, as cited in Ratner, *Taxation and Democracy,* p. 261.

54. Stephen Diamond, "Citizenship, Civilization, and Coercion: Justice Holmes on the Tax Power," in *The Legacy of Oliver Wendell Holmes Jr.,* ed. Robert W. Gordon (Stanford, Calif.: Stanford University Press, 1992), p. 150.

55. Ratner, *Taxation and Democracy,* pp. 286–304.

56. Ibid., p. 314.

57. Franklin D. Roosevelt, "Message to Congress on Tax Revision," June 19, 1935.

58. Ratner, *Taxation and Democracy,* p. 354.

59. Representative Joseph W. Bailey, from Ratner, *Taxation and Democracy,* p. 279.

60. Ratner, *Taxation and Democracy,* p. 348.

61. Ibid., p. 272.

62. Ibid., p. 297.

63. Ibid., p. 380. Calculation based on using the inflation calculator at the Bureau of Labor Statistics (*www.bls.gov*).

64. Witte, *Politics and Development,* p. 86.

65. Ratner, *Taxation and Democracy,* p. 375. It is worth noting that the war was still largely financed by $15 billion in loans, in comparison with $4 billion in tax revenue, which was still highly regressive.

66. Andrew Mellon, *Taxation: The People's Business* (New York: Macmillan, 1924), pp. 56–57.

67. Ratner, *Taxation and Democracy,* p. 397.

68. Chernow, *Titan,* p. 624.

69. Ratner, *Taxation and Democracy,* p. 449.

70. Ibid., p. 415.

71. *Congressional Record,* 70th Cong., 1st sess., 69:641; also *American Economic Review* 18:439. Ratner, *Taxation and Democracy,* pp. 432–33.

72. Witte, *Politics and Development,* pp. 93–95.

73. Franklin D. Roosevelt, Message to Congress, January 1935.

74. Ratner, *Taxation and Democracy,* p. 471.

75. Witte, *Politics and Development,* p. 100. Paraphrased in John Morton Blum,

From the Morgenthau Diaries: Years of Crisis, 1928–1938 (Boston: Houghton Mifflin, 1959), p. 301.

76. Blum, *Morgenthau Diaries*, p. 303. For a good discussion of FDR's 1935 tax program, see Kennedy, *Freedom from Fear*, pp. 275–77.

77. Ratner, *Taxation and Democracy*, p. 471.

78. Attorney Jonathon Blattmachr notes that the sole reason this proposal was advanced was because of lobbying by the rich. Letter to authors, May 22, 2002.

79. Iris J. Lav and Joel Friedman, "Can Capital Gains Carry-Over Basis Replace the Estate Tax?" (Washington, D.C.: Center on Budget and Policy Priorities, March 15, 2001).

80. Our friend Jon Blattmachr disagrees with this point. He points to the Canadian experience; Canada adopted a capital gains at death system in 1971. See Jonathon Blattmachr, *Wealth Preservation for Closely Held Business Owners* (Washington, D.C.: Regnery Press, 1998); and Jonathon Blattmachr, *Wealth Preservation and Estate Planning* (Washington, D.C.: Regnery Publishing, 2000).

81. Lav and Friedman, "Capital Gains Carry-over." Also see William Gale and Joel Slemrod, "Overview," in *Rethinking Estate and Gift Taxation,* ed. William Gale, James R. Hines Jr., and Joel Slemrod (Washington, D.C.: Brookings Institution Press, 2001), pp. 15, 195, 209.

82. Jon Blattmachr, letter to authors, May 25, 2002.

3. Opposition to the Estate Tax

1. The advertisement was in the *Washington Times,* March 15, 2001, p. A7. Erin O'Leary would not return calls for an interview.

2. Birnbaum and Murray, *Showdown at Gucci Gulch.*

3. See Richard W. Stevenson, "Quiet on Lobbying Front: Sudden Halt to Coalition's Bid for Corporate Tax Breaks," *New York Times,* February 23, 2001; Jill Abramson, "Lobbyists Waiting on the Levy for Their Ship to Come In," *New York Times,* March 4, 2001.

4. Ernst & Young was the number one largest contributor to Representative Cox's campaign and the third-largest contributor to Representative Dunn's according to the Center on Responsive Politics in 1997 and 1998 (*www.opensecrets.org*).

5. Lizette Alvarez, "Capitol Hill Memo: In Two Parties War of Words, Shibboleths Emerge as Clear Winner," *New York Times,* April 27, 2001.

6. Jonathon Weisman, "Linking Tax to Death May Have Brought Its Doom," *USA Today,* May 21, 2001.

7. Leonard Goldberg, Californians for Tax Reform, interview, January 2, 2002.

8. Christopher Cox, letter to the editor, *USA Today,* June 1, 2001.

9. Andrea Billups, "Bush Pal Around for Long Haul," *Washington Times,* August 11, 2001.

10. Joshua Green, "Meet Mr. Death," *American Prospect,* May 21, 2001, p. 12.

11. From the Web site of Cymric and the personal biography of Patricia M. Soldano, *www.cymricfamilyoffice.com/experience,* October 10, 2001.

12. Ibid.

13. Disclosure information for 1997 and 1998 for both Patricia Soldano and the Policy and Taxation Group is located at the Center for Responsible Politics, Open Secrets database, compiled using lobby disclosure reports as required under the Lobbying Disclosure Act of 1995. Lobbying income in 1998 was $266,000. Thirty thousand dollars came from Mars Inc. in 1998 and fifty thousand dollars in 1997. From *www.opensecrets.org.* Reviewed June 24, 2002.

14. Patton Boggs information from the Center for Responsible Politics, Open Secrets database, compiled using lobby disclosure reports as required under the Lobbying Disclosure Act of 1995. Senators informed us that they were being heavily lobbied on estate tax repeal by representatives of Mars Inc., which paid Patton Boggs $640,000 in 1997, $700,000 in 1998, $620,000 in 1999, and $720,000 in 2000. From *www.opensecrets.org/lobbyists,* downloaded and updated June 24, 2002.

15. The "Gallo amendment" is discussed in Birnbaum and Murray, *Showdown at Gucci Gulch,* p. 140.

16. Legislative history compiled from Web resources from the U.S. House of Representatives, *www.house.gov.*

17. *Simpson's Contemporary Quotations,* compiled by James B. Simpson (Boston: Houghton Mifflin, 1988), no. 8234 (as located on *www.bartleby.com*). Originally we thought the quote was from A. J. Leibling (who said "Freedom of the press is guaranteed only to those who own one"), but after consulting a number of quote search engines, we found the quote attributed to former AFL-CIO president Lane Kirkland. The full colorful quote is "My pappy told me never to bet my bladder against a brewery or get into an argument with people who buy ink by the barrel."

18. Newsmakers, "One Publisher's Taxing Crusade," *Brills Content,* June 2001.

19. Ibid.

20. The *Seattle Times* Web site, *www.deathtax.com,* posted these newsletters, including memos circulated to the members and allies of the Pacific Northwest Newspaper Association. This claim was made in the April 15, 1998, newsletter.

21. Newsmakers, "One Publisher's Taxing Crusade," p. 114.

22. "Death tax newsletter," *www.deathtax.com,* dated March 29, 2001, downloaded August 13, 2001.

23. "Death tax newsletter," *www.deathtax.com,* dated October 21, 1998, downloaded August 13, 2001.

24. Ibid.

25. Newsmakers, "One Publisher's Taxing Crusade."

26. Ibid.

27. David Cay Johnston, "Talk of Lost Farms Reflects Muddle of Estate Tax Debate," *New York Times,* April 8, 2001.

28. Quote from Senator Grassley in Johnston, "Talk of Lost Farms."

29. Johnston, "Talk of Lost Farms."

30. Gless Kessler, "Estate Tax Repeal Bill Delivered," *Washington Post,* August 25, 2000.

31. "Remarks by the President on Veto of Death Tax Elimination Act of 2000," Office of the Press Secretary, the White House, August 31, 2000.

32. Gless Kessler, "Estate Tax Repeal."

33. Ibid. Also see Neil Harl, "Does Farm and Ranch Property Need a Federal Estate and Gift Tax Rate?" *Tax Notes* 68, no. 7 (August 14, 1995): 875–77.

34. Lloyd Brown of Hertz management, from David Cay Johnston, "Talk of Lost Farms."

35. Johnston, "Talk of Lost Farms."

36. An article in the *Bulletin Frontrunner* notes that the federation, stung by an April 8 *New York Times* article reporting that the federation could not cite a single example of a farm lost because of the estate taxes, put out an all-points bulletin on April 19. *Congressional Quarterly* added that "as of Tuesday, the Farm Bureau had not yet received any examples according to spokesman Don Lipton." From "Farm Bureau Finding Difficulty in Documenting Effects of Estate Tax," *Bulletin Frontrunner,* April 25, 2001.

37. William Gale and Joel Slemrod, "Rhetoric and Economics in the Estate Tax Debate," a paper prepared for the National Tax Association Spring Symposium, final draft, May 22, 2001, p. 12.

38. Johnston, "Talk of Lost Farms."

39. Besides the effective exemption that everyone gets ($1 million in 2002), the 1997 reform of the estate tax permits a special deduction (which combined with an effective exemption removed $1.3 million from taxation prior to the 2001 reforms and would allow much more today). This special deduction is for

family–owned farms and businesses when they constitute at least 50 percent of an estate and in which heirs materially participate. Taxpayers are also allowed to value real estate on the basis of current-use value rather than market value. This can reduce the value of the taxable gross estate by up to $770,000 for decedents who died in 2000.

40. Johnston, "Talk of Lost Farms."

41. The Federal Agricultural Improvement and Reform Act was passed in March 1996 by a margin of 74 to 26 in the Senate and 318 to 89 in the House. Of the fifty-one senators supporting estate tax repeal who were in the Senate in 1996, forty-nine of them voted for the legislation. Senator Blanche Lincoln (D-Ark.) was the only pro-repeal senator who opposed the bill in 1996. Research conducted by Chris Hartman, United for a Fair Economy, 2001.

42. Ben Lilliston and Neil Ritchie, "Freedom to Fail: How U.S. Farming Policies Have Helped Agribusiness and Pushed Family Farmers Toward Extinction," *Multinational Monitor* 21, no. 7 & 8 (July/August 2000).

43. Statistic according to Willard Cochrane, professor emeritus at the University of Minnesota, as cited in Lilliston and Ritchie, "Freedom to Fail."

44. Ibid.

45. According to the Environmental Working Group, the 2002 farm bill is even more skewed, with over 80 percent of the subsidies going to the top 10 percent of farms and ranches. See *www.ewg.org*.

46. Review and Outlook, "Prairie Plutocrats," *Wall Street Journal,* February 1, 2002.

47. Chuck Hassebrook, "Lower Estate Taxes Will Hurt Small Farms," *New York Times,* July 15, 1997.

48. Lawrence Goodwyn, *Democratic Promise: The Populist Moment in America* (New York: Oxford University Press, 1976); and Michael Kazin, *Populist Persuasion: An American History* (New York: HarperCollins, 1995).

49. David Cay Johnston, "Despite Benefits, Democrats' Estate Tax Plan Gets Little Notice," *New York Times,* July 13, 2000.

50. Ibid.

51. The most important reform amendments were offered by several North Dakota legislators: Senator Kent Conrad, Senator Byron Dorgan, and Representative Earl Pomeroy in the House.

52. Environmental Working Group Farm Subsidy Database (*www.ewg.org*), updated on May 6, 2002. Also noted in Review and Outlook, "Prairie Plutocrats," *Wall Street Journal,* February 1, 2002.

53. On WBUR's nationally syndicated program "The Connection," Cornwell

admitted that he grazes a substantial amount of cattle on federal land and benefits from grazing subsidies, February 19, 2001.

54. "Western Land Management: Subsidized Cow Chow," *The Economist,* March 9, 2002.

55. Associated Press State and Local Wire, "Few Pay Estate Taxes in Montana," July 28, 2000.

56. These numbers were provided by Senator Conrad Burns of Montana, a proponent of complete repeal. As cited in Associated Press State and Local Wire, "Few Pay Estate Taxes."

57. Judy Xanthopoulos, Quantria Strategies, LLC, Washington, D.C., based on 1999 IRS data and rate structures based on 2009 current estate law. Also see Iris J. Lav, "Estate Tax Repeal and the Top Income Tax Rate Cut: A State-by-State Look at Who Would Benefit," May 14, 2001.

58. According to the *Seattle Times,* Blethen's ownership stake in that newspaper is "over $400 million." The value of the Blethen newspapers overall is estimated at $1 billion. "The *Seattle Times* is a family-controlled business with assets valued at more than $400 million." John Hendren and Kevin Galvin, "Gates Sr. Says His Son Shouldn't Get Tax Break," *Seattle Times,* March 16, 2001.

59. Numbers for everyone but Frank Blethen come from "The 400 Richest People in America," *Forbes,* October 8, 2001.

60. Joint Economic Committee, "The Economics of the Estate Tax," December 1998, *www.house.gov/jec.*

61. Ibid.

62. Jim Hopkins, "Family Firms Confront Calamities of Transfer without Plans, Next Generation Faces Stifling Tax Burden," *USA Today,* August 29, 2000.

63. James Repetti, quoted in "The Thorniest Tax," *Advisor Today* (Bell & Howell Information and Learning), June 2000.

64. Charles Davenport and Jay A. Soled, "Enlivening the Death-Tax Death-Talk," *Tax Notes,* July 26, 1999, special report, pp. 591–630.

65. Douglas Holt-Eakin, John W. Phillips, and Harvey S. Rosen, "Estate Taxes, Life Insurance, and Small Business," working paper 7360 (Cambridge, Mass.: National Bureau of Economic Research, 1999), cited in Gale and Slemrod, "Overview," p. 47.

66. For instance, researchers omit life insurance held in trusts, nonfinancial assets, and balances in 401(k)s or other pension accounts, each of which would raise available resources with which to pay estate taxes. See Gale and Slemrod, "Overview," p. 47.

67. Gale and Slemrod, "Overview," p. 47.

68. Ibid., p. 48.

69. Matthew Pinzur, "Estate Tax Seldom an Issue for Most," *Florida Times Union,* September 20, 2000.

70. CNN *Crossfire,* March 14, 2001.

71. Center on Tax Policy Web site (*www.policyandtaxationgroup.com*), downloaded August 17, 2001.

72. Gale and Slemrod, "Overview," p. 32. William Gale is the first person we heard use the phrase "death bonus."

73. Gale and Slemrod, "Rhetoric and Economics," pp. 18–19.

74. Ibid., p. 3.

75. Taxes imposed at death do not distort people's lifetime job and income decisions and saving behavior compared with taxes that are imposed on wages or assets while people are alive. Taxes on the living reduce consumption, saving, and economic choices and might change individual behaviors that are not always best for the individual or society. But after a person dies—well, the tax cannot interfere with the way he or she was able to live. The lives of the heirs will be affected by the tax, but not significantly, because the tax is paid before they have the money.

76. "Who Pays?" Institute for Taxation and Economic Policy, 1995.

77. Liam Murphy and Thomas Nagel, *The Myth of Ownership: Taxes and Justice* (New York: Oxford University Press, 2002), pp. 14647.

78. Patricia Soldano and the Policy and Taxation Group, "Reasons to Eliminate the Federal Estate Tax,"—*www.taxandpolicygroup.com,* downloaded August 17, 2001.

79. Advertisement, "African American Business Leaders Call for an End to the Estate Tax," *New York Times,* April 4, 2001, p. C3.

80. Julianne Malveaux, "The Crassness of Class," *Sun Reporter,* April 12, 2001.

81. Gale and Slemrod, "Overview," p. 48. Gale and Slemrod conclude, "A significant portion of the value of family-owned businesses consists of unrealized capital gains." Arthur Kennickell and David Wilcox ("The Value and Distribution of Unrealized Capital Gains: Evidence from the 1989 Survey of Consumer Finances" [Washington, D.C.: Federal Reserve Board (mimeo), 1992]) peg the figure at two-thirds using the 1989 Survey of Consumer Finance. Evidence in James Poterba and Scott Weisbrenner ("The Distributional Burden of Taxing Estates and Unrealized Capital Gains at Death," in *Rethinking Estate and Gift Taxation,* ed. William Gale, James R. Hines Jr., and Joel Slemrod (Washington, D.C.: Brookings Institution Press, 2001]) suggests that the figure was 80 percent

in 1998. This income has never been taxed under the income tax and would never be taxed at all if exempted from the estate tax."

82. Joseph J. Cordes and C. Eugene Steuele, "Death, Taxes and Charity," *Foundation News and Commentary* 40, no. 5 (September/October 1999).

83. Murphy and Nagel, *Myth of Ownership,* p. 143.

84. Internal Revenue Service, Statistics of Income Division, unpublished data, revised May 2001.

85. See Blattmachr, *Wealth Preservation for Closely Held Business Owners;* and Blattmachr, *Wealth Preservation and Estate Planning.*

86. James Poterba, "The Estate Tax and After-Tax Investment Returns," working paper series 98–11 (University of Michigan, Office of Tax Policy Research, 1998), as cited in Gale and Slemrod, "Overview," p. 151.

87. From the Web site of the Center on Taxation and Policy, *www.taxandpolicygroup.com,* downloaded August 17, 2001.

88. Newsmakers, "One Publisher's Taxing Crusade."

89. Gale and Slemrod, "Overview," pp. 37–38.

90. Ibid.

91. Ibid.

92. Ibid., p. 39.

93. Davenport and Soled, "Enlivening the Death-Tax Death-Talk," *Tax Notes,* July 26, 1999, special report, pp. 591–630, cited in Gale and Slemrod, "Overview," pp. 38–39. This is based on taking one–half of the total lawyer's fees and other costs reported on estate tax returns and reducing that number by 45 percent to reflect tax deductibility of costs. *Note:* That last reduction is inappropriate for measuring the social rather than private costs of the activity—you could make an argument about the opportunity costs and social inefficiency of so many people engaged in avoidance. Also see Gale and Slemrod, "Rhetoric and Economics," pp. 18–19.

94. James R. Repetti, "The Case for the Estate and Gift Tax," *Tax Notes,* March 13, 2000, pp. 1493–1510.

95. Joel Slemrod and Nikki Sorum, "The Compliance Cost of the U.S. Individual Income Tax System," *National Tax Journal* 37 (December 1984): 461–74. Marsha Blumenthal and Joel Slemrod, "The Income Tax Compliance of Big Business," *Public Finance Quarterly* 24 (October 1996): 411–38.

96. Marsha Blumenthal and Joel Slemrod, "The Compliance Cost of the U.S. Individual Income Tax: A Second Look after Tax Reform," *National Tax Journal* 45 (June 1992): 185–202.

97. "Reasons the Death Tax Does Not Work," from the Web site of the Center

markdownotnavNOTES TO PAGES 90–97   *157*

for Taxation and Policy, *www.policyandtaxationgroup.com*, downloaded August 17, 2001.

98. For international comparisons, see Wolff, *Top Heavy*. Also see OECD Tax Policy Studies #6, "Tax and the Economy: A Comparative Assessment of OECD countries (Paris: OECD, 2001).

99. CNN *Crossfire*, March 14, 2001.

100. The Dirksen Congressional Center gets many inquires about the origins of this quote attributed to Everett Dirksen. On its Web site is a two-page discussion of whether he actually did say it. But he said a number of things very close to this famous quote, and several claim to have heard it in his speeches, though no written record exists. See *www.pekin.net/dirksen/featuresBillionHere.htm*.

101. Gale and Potter, "Economic Evaluation."

4. The Showdown

1. Lynn Asinof and Tom Herman, "On Bush's List: The Estate Tax Could Become a Central Issue," *Wall Street Journal*, December 14, 2000.

2. Thanks to researcher Matt Hamill for clarifying this process.

3. Robert Greenstein, "Can the New Surplus Projections Accommodate a Large Tax Cut?" Center on Budget and Policy Priorities, *www.cbpp.org*, January 4, 2001.

4. Ibid.

5. Warren Rudman, Robert Rubin, Paul Volcker, Pete Peterson, and the Concord Coalition, "On Taxes, One Step at a Time," *Washington Post*, April 4, 2001.

6. "Selling the Tax Cut," *Business Week*, February 5, 2001.

7. Steve Liesman, "Bush's $1.6 Trillion Tax Cut May Not Deliver Right Fix: Some Economists Dislike Using Fiscal Measures to Prop Up Economy," *Wall Street Journal*, January 8, 2001.

8. John D. McKinnon, "Repeal of Estate Tax Ranks as Priority, but Effects Wouldn't Be Felt Soon," *Wall Street Journal*, January 8, 2001.

9. Paul Krugman, *Fuzzy Math: The Essential Guide to the Bush Tax Plan* (New York: Norton, 2001), pp. 17–19.

10. Shailagh Murray and John D. McKinnon, "GOP Senators Push for Quick Tax Cut atop Bush Package to Rouse Economy," *Wall Street Journal*, March 23, 2001.

11. Ibid.

12. "Remarks by the President During Meeting with Small Business Owners," the White House, March 16, 2001.

13. Washington Wire, "Lawmakers Scramble for Position amid Talk of Speeding Up Tax Cuts," *Wall Street Journal,* March 23, 2001. Also see the Institute on Taxation and Economic Policy, which found that only 1 percent of small business owners paid the 39.6 percent rate. We can draw the conclusion that six thousand to eight thousand small business owners would benefit from the rate reduction, not 17.4 million! The Center on Budget and Policy Priorities, examining 1997 data, found that a total of 691,000 individuals were subject to the top tax rate. These include many who are not small business owners—professional athletes and entertainers, wealth investors, corporate executives. "About One Percent of Small Business Owners Pay 39.6 Percent Tax Rate," Center on Budget and Policy Priorities, *www.cbpp.org,* March 28, 2001.

14. "Defending the Estate Tax," *New York Times,* February 16, 2001.

15. David Cay Johnston, "Some Experts Questioning Bush Plan on Estate Taxes," *New York Times,* January 29, 2001.

16. Ibid.

17. Douglas Freeman, a California estate tax planner, said, "The analysis done by the tax-writing committee staff of the cost of repeal has been very poor and shows they have not given much thought, if any, to how repeal will affect the income tax" or to "creative ways that will be found to cut the income tax bills of the wealthy." From Johnston, "Some Experts Questioning Bush Plan."

18. John D. McKinnon, "Repeal of Estate Tax Would Cost More Than Previous Estimates," *Wall Street Journal,* March 27, 2001.

19. Ibid. Also memo from Al Davis, John Buckley, Ways and Means Democratic staff, dated March 27, 2001, and testimony before the House Committee on Ways and Means by Lauren Y. Detzel, attorney with Dean Mead Egerton Bloodworth Capauano & Bozrath, P.A., Orlando, Florida, March 21, 2001.

20. Quoted in "The Thorniest Tax."

21. Elizabeth Becker, "Bush Aide Faults Plan to Repeal Estate Tax," *New York Times,* February 10, 2001.

22. In the summer of 2000, United for a Fair Economy worked hard to ensure that there were adequate votes in the House of Representatives to be able to uphold President Clinton's veto. Although many key constituencies found it hard to mobilize during August, we were able to switch a dozen votes. The margin to protect the veto was much closer than anyone would have liked.

23. Center on Budget and Policy Priorities, "4,500 Largest Estates Would Receive as Much from Bush Tax Plan as 142 Million Americans," *www.cbpp.org,* February 26, 2001.

24. Former senator Alan Simpson, "Testimony Submitted to the Subcommittee on Taxation and IRS Oversight," March 15, 2001.

25. Americans for Sensible Estate Tax Solutions, "Reforming the Estate Tax," a policy paper, March 2001.

26. Simpson, "Testimony Submitted."

27. David Cay Johnston, "Dozens of Rich Americans Join in Fight to Retain the Estate Tax," *New York Times,* February 14, 2001.

28. Joan Walsh, "Plutocrats to the Rescue," *www.Salon.com,* February 15, 2001.

29. Thanks to Bill Gale from the Brookings Institution for this humorous observation.

30. Jane Bryant Quinn, "Tax Cuts: Who Will Get What?" *Newsweek,* June 11, 2001.

31. Joel Friedman, Richard Kogan, and Robert Greenstein, "New Tax-Cut Law Ultimately Costs as Much as Bush Plan: Gimmicks Used to Camouflage $4.1 Trillion Cost in Second Decade," Center on Budget and Policy Priorities, *www.cbpp.org,* June 27, 2001.

32. Gale and Potter, "Economic Evaluation."

33. Citizens for Tax Justice, "The Final Bush Tax Plan: An Overview of Round One," *Citizens for Tax Justice,* June 2001.

34. Ibid.

35. Friedman, Kogan, and Greenstein, "New Tax-Cut Law."

36. Gale and Potter, "Economic Evaluation," p. 16.

37. Section 2057 of the IRS Code. Also see Gale and Potter, "Economic Evaluation," p. 16.

38. Jon Blattmachr, correspondence with authors, May 25, 2002.

39. Iris Lav and Joel Friedman, "Can Capital Gains Carry-Over Basis Replace the Estate Tax?" Center on Budget and Policy Priorities, *www.cbpp.org,* March 15, 2001.

40. The conservation easement is extended so that any property in the United States or any possession of the United States can now be set aside for the purpose of conservation, thereby reducing the total value of the estate. The prior law required that land be within a certain distance of a national park or wilderness area or urban national forest to be considered. This provision was made retroactive to January 1, 2001, and we think it is a positive change in the estate tax.

41. Quinn, "Tax Cuts."

42. Ibid.

43. Krugman, "Bad Heir Day."

44. Patricia Soldano, "Status of Current Activities as of June 1, 2001," Policy and Taxation Group Web site (*www.policyandtaxationgroup.com*), downloaded August 17, 2001.

45. Brandes, *Warhogs.*

5. What We Owe Our Society

1. FDR quote from Witte, *Politics and Development,* p. 66.

2. United for a Fair Economy, "Born on Third Base: The Source of Wealth of the 1997 Forbes 400" (Boston: United for a Fair Economy, 1997). Figures for 1999 based on "The Forbes 400," *Forbes,* September 28, 1999.

3. Tyco International's CEO L. Dennis Kozlowski received a pay package of $170 million in 1999, which made him the second-highest paid CEO on *Business Week*'s annual list. Quote from Jennifer Reingold, "Executive Pay: Special Report," *Business Week,* April 17, 2000, p. 108.

4. David Cay Johnston, "You Can't Take It with You," *New York Times Review of Books,* April 21, 2001.

5. Berkshire Hathaway annual meeting, Omaha, 1996, as cited in Janet Lowe, *Warren Buffett Speaks: Wit and Wisdom from the World's Greatest Investor* (New York: Wiley, 1997), p. 164.

6. "Warren Buffett Talks Business," University of North Carolina, Center for Public Television, Chapel Hill, 1995. (Modified later by Buffett letter to author), as cited in Lowe, *Warren Buffett Speaks,* p. 164.

7. Hernando deSoto, *The Mystery of Capital: Why Capitalism Triumphs in the West and Fails Everywhere Else* (New York: Basic Books, 2000).

8. Ibid., p. 15.

9. Ibid., p. 52.

10. Peter Barnes, *Who Owns the Sky?* (Washington, D.C.: Island Press, 2001), p. 118.

11. This section is greatly indebted to a terrific book, Joseph William Singer's *The Edges of the Field: Lessons on the Obligations of Ownership* (Boston: Beacon Press, 2000). It was through Singer's work that we identified some of the source material on Islam and Judaism for this section.

12. Meir Tamari, *The Challenge of Wealth: A Jewish Perspective on Earning and Spending Money* (Northvale, N.J.: Jason Aronson, 1995), p. xxiii.

13. Ibid., p. 128.

14. Ibid., p. 148.

15. Singer, *Edges of the Field,* p. 60.

16. Ibid., p. 59. Peter J. Gomes, *The Good Book: Reading the Bible with Mind and Heart* (New York: Avon Books, 1996), pp. 287, 306–8.

17. National Conference of Catholic Bishops, *Economic Justice for All: Pastoral Letter on Catholic Social Teaching and the U.S. Economy* (Washington, D.C.: National Conference of Catholic Bishops, 1986), section 115, p. 58.

18. Ibid., section 113, p. 57.

19. Pope John Paul II, *Laborem Exercens (On Human Work),* September 14, 1981, section 12.

20. Berkshire Hathaway annual report, Omaha, 1994, cited in Lowe, *Warren Buffett Speaks,* p. 168.

21. "Warren Buffett Talks Business," as cited in Lowe, *Warren Buffett Speaks,* p. 164.

22. Edward Cohen, "The Estate Tax and Charity," Web site sponsored by Commonwealth: Nonprofits, Philanthropy, and Civil Society, *www.epn.commonwealth.com,* downloaded January 11, 2001.

23. Alexis de Toqueville, *Democracy in America,* ed. J. P. Mayer (New York: Harper & Row, 1969), 2:287.

24. Ibid., 2:513.

25. Ibid., 2:514.

26. Robert D. Putnam, *Bowling Alone: The Collapse and Revival of American Community* (New York: Touchstone Books, 2001).

27. John DiIulio Jr., Remarks at the Religious Action Center Conference, March 13, 2001. Copyright 2001, eMediaMillWorks, Inc f/k/a Federal Document Clearing House, Inc.

28. For information on the historical impact of the Rockefeller Foundation, see Raymond B. Fosdick, *The Story of the Rockefeller Foundation* (New Brunswick, N.J.: Transaction, 1989).

29. Jim Grote, "Win, Lose, or Draw?" *www.MorningstarAdvisor.com,* September 13, 2000.

30. George Soros, "Kill the Death Tax Now . . . No, Keep It Alive to Help the Needy," *Wall Street Journal,* July 14, 2000.

31. In 2000, over $210 billion was given to charity. In 2001, the amount exceeded $212 billion, and the amount given by individuals was roughly three-quarters of this amount. Stephanie Strom, "Charitable Contributions in 2001 Reached $212 Billion," *New York Times,* June 21, 2002.

32. OMB Watch analysis of IRS charitable data. "The Estate Tax and Charitable Giving," *www.ombwatch.org,* March 2001.

33. David Joulfaian, "Charitable Giving in Life and Death," in *Rethinking Estate and Gift Taxation*, ed. William Gale, James R. Hines Jr., and Joel Slemrod (Washington, D.C.: Brookings Institution Press, 2001), p. 361.

34. IRS data as cited in OMB Watch, "The Estate Tax and Charitable Giving," *www.ombwatch.org*, March 2001. An estimated 25 percent goes to other charities not covered in these major categories, including social services.

35. Mary Jacoby, "Will Charitable Giving Fall If Estate Tax Does?" *St. Petersburg Times*, May 14, 2001.

36. Stuart Butler, "Why the Bush Tax Cuts Are No Threat to Philanthropy," *Heritage Foundation Reports*, Heritage Foundation, March 8, 2001.

37. Paul G. Schervish, "Philanthropy Can Thrive without Estate Tax," *Chronicle of Philanthropy*, January 11, 2001. The quotes that follow are from this article.

38. "The Impact of Tax Restructuring on Tax Exempt Organizations," was a study conducted by the Washington National Tax Service of Price Waterhouse LLP and the law firm of Caplin and Drysdale in April 1997.

39. OMB Watch, "The Estate Tax and Charitable Giving," *www.ombwatch.org*, downloaded November 15, 2001. Extrapolation based on 1999 data.

40. U.S. Treasury Department, series of studies about the effects of the estate tax on charity: Gerald Auten and David Joulfaian, "Charitable Contributions and Intergenerational Transfers," February 1996; and David Joulfaian, "The Federal Estate and Gift Tax: Description, Profile of Taxpayers, and Economic Consequences," December 1998. These studies are available in PDF format from *www.treasury.gov*.

41. An earlier study concludes: "The deductibility of bequests has a significant effect on such transfers. . . . Overall, however, the estate tax has a modest effect on giving. . . . In absence of the estate tax, the above findings suggest that charitable bequests may decline by about 12 percent." Joulfaian, "Estate Taxes and Charitable Bequests by the Wealthy," working paper 7663, National Bureau of Economic Research, April 2000.

42. John J. Havens and Paul Schervish, "Millionaires and the Millennium: New Estimates of the Forthcoming Wealth Transfer and the Prospects for a Golden Age of Philanthropy," Boston College Social Welfare Research Institute, October 19, 1999.

43. Carnegie, *Gospel of Wealth*, p. 20.

44. Ibid.

45. Ibid., p. 21.

46. William D. Danko and Thomas J. Stanley, *The Millionaire Next Door* (New York: Pocket Books, 1996); thanks to Jim Grote for bringing this to our attention.

47. Ibid., p. 146.

48. Ibid., p. 170.

49. Roger Lowenstein, *Buffett: The Making of an American Capitalist* (New York: Doubleday, 1996).

50. Repetti, "Democracy, Taxes and Wealth."

51. John M. Keynes, *The Collected Writings of John Maynard Keynes* (London: Royal Economic Society, 1972), p. 299.

Epilogue: The Estate Tax and the Common Good

1. Xanthopoulos, *Quantria Strategies,* based on 1999 IRS data and rate structures based on 2009 current estate law. Also see Lav, "Estate Tax Repeal."

SELECTED BIBLIOGRAPHY

An expanded bibliography is available at www.responsiblewealth.org/commonwealth

Barnes, Peter. *Who Owns the Sky?* (Washington, D.C.: Island Press, 2001).

Birnbaum, Jeffrey H., and Alan S. Murray. *Showdown at Gucci Gulch: Lawyers, Lobbyists, and the Unlikely Triumph of Tax Reform* (New York: Random House, 1987).

Brandes, Stuart D. *Warhogs: A History of War Profits in America* (Lexington, Ky.: University Press of Kentucky, 1997).

Carnegie, Andrew. *The Gospel of Wealth and Other Timely Essays.* Ed. Edward C. Kirkland (Cambridge, Mass.: The Belknap Press of Harvard University, 1962).

Chernow, Ron. *Titan: The Life of John D. Rockefeller* (New York: Random House, 1998).

———. *The House of Morgan: An American Banking Dynasty and the Rise of Modern Finance* (New York: Simon & Schuster, 1990).

Collins, Chuck, and Felice Yeskel. *Economic Apartheid in America: A Primer on Economic Inequality and Insecurity* (New York: The New Press, 2000).

de Soto, Hernando. *The Mystery of Capital: Why Capitalism Triumphs in the West and Fails Everywhere Else* (New York: Basic Books, 2000).

Gale, William G., et al., eds. *Rethinking Estate and Gift Taxation* (Washington, D.C.: Brookings Institution, 2001).

Gates, Jeff. *The Ownership Solution: Toward a Shared Capitalism for the Twenty-first Century* (Reading, Mass.: Addison Wesley, 1998).

———. *Democracy at Risk: Rescuing Main Street from Wall Street* (Cambridge, Mass.: Perseus Books, 2000).

Huston, James L. *Securing the Fruits of Labor: The American Concept of Wealth Distribution, 1765–1900* (Baton Rouge, La.: University of Louisiana Press, 1998).

Keister, Lisa A. *Wealth in America: Trends in Wealth Inequality* (Cambridge, Eng.: Cambridge University Press, 2000).

Kennedy, David. *Freedom from Fear: The American People in Depression and War, 1929–1945* (New York: Oxford University Press, 1999).

Krugman, Paul. *Fuzzy Math: The Essential Guide to the Bush Tax Plan* (New York: Norton, 2001).

McCullough, David. *John Adams* (New York: Simon & Schuster, 2001).

Morris, Edmund. *Theodore Rex* (New York: Random House, 2001).

Murphy, Liam, and Thomas Nagel. *The Myth of Ownership: Taxes and Justice* (New York: Oxford University Press, 2002).

Paine, Thomas. *Common Sense* (New York: Barnes and Noble Books, 1995).

Phillips, Kevin. *Wealth and Democracy: A Political History of the American Rich* (New York: Broadway Books, 2002).

Putnam, Robert D. *Bowling Alone: The Collapse and Revival of American Community* (New York: Touchstone Books, 2001).

Ratner, Sidney. *Taxation and Democracy in America.* Rev. ed. (New York: John Wiley & Sons, Inc., 1967).

Singer, Joseph William. *The Edges of the Field: Lessons on the Obligations of Ownership* (Boston: Beacon Press, 2000).

Stanley, Thomas J., and William D. Danko. *The Millionaire Next Door: The Suprising Secrets of America's Wealthy* (New York: Simon & Schuster, 1996).

Witte, John F. *The Politics and Development of the Federal Income Tax* (Madison, Wis.: University of Wisconsin Press, 1985).

Wolff, Edward N. *Top Heavy: The Increasing Inequality of Wealth in America and What Can Be Done about It* (New York: The New Press, 2002).

ACKNOWLEDGMENTS

This book is about the many factors that go into the creation of
wealth, beyond an individual's effort. The same is true of a writing
project. It takes a village to write a book.

We are greatly indebted to people who have done research,
writing, and advocacy on the estate tax issue. Many of these patri-
ots are acknowledged in our footnotes, but a special thanks goes to
William Gale at the Brookings Institution for his contribution.

We are very appreciative of the people who helped with re-
search, editing, and other details, including Chris Hartman, Mark
Roberts, Randy Oftedahl, Rosie Hunter, Jessie Schnapp, Lynn
Mercer, and Tina Frank.

Thanks to those readers who gave us insightful comments and
corrections, including: Gary Bass, Jonathan Blattmachr, Sidney
and Betty Carroll, Edward Collins, Deborah Holzman, Meizhu
Lui, Sam Pizzigati, Jean Strouse, and Jennifer Troobnick. Thanks
to Andrew Boyd for his suggestions about the title.

Gratitude to the entire board and staff of Responsible Wealth
and United for a Fair Economy for making some of the history recounted in these pages. A special thanks to Chris Hartman, Karen
Kraut, Scott Klinger, Mike Lapham, Meizhu Lui, Mike Miller,
Sam Pizzigati, and Pam Rogers.

The team at Beacon Press has been a joy to work with at every
stage. Special thanks to Helene Atwan, Tom Hallock, Pam Mac-
Coll, Deb Chasman, and Mary Ray Worley.

Our appreciation to Mesa Refuge for providing sanctuary for
research, reading, and writing. Novenas to Tricia Brennan and
Nora Collins for the sanctuary at home.

166